RUDIMENTS OF MUSIC

by

STEWART MACPHERSON
1865 — 1941

New edition, 1970

With a new chapter by Anthony Payne

Standard Book Number 852 49010 0

D1288939

© 1939, 1970 Galliard Ltd

GALLIARD LTD
New York: GALAXY MUSIC CORPORATION

TABLE OF CONTENTS

RUDIMENTS OF MUSIC

___

INTRODUCTION

1 —Musical sound is the result of regular and periodic vibrations of air.

2 —The varying height or depth of sound is caused by the difference of the rapidity of these vibrations, and is called the pitch of the sound.

3 —The loudness or softness of a sound depends upon the size, or amplitude, of the vibrations.

4 —The quality (or *timbre*) of a sound depends upon the nature of the vibrating body (i.e., the medium by which vibration is set up, whether string or column of air); and also upon the presence, in greater or less degree, of harmonics. (See Table of Definitions.)

5 —The indication, in writing, of musical sounds requires:—
    (i.) Notes—to express duration.
    (ii.) The staff, or stave } to express pitch.
    (iii.) Clefs

___

CHAPTER I.

DURATION OF SOUNDS—NOTES

1.—The relative duration of musical sounds is made clear to the eye by signs of varying shape called notes.

2.—Those now commonly in use are as follows:—

‖o‖ ,		Breve.
o ,		Semibreve, or whole-note.
♩ , or	♩	Minim, or half-note.
♩ , or	♩	Crotchet, or quaver-note.
♪ , or	♪	Quaver, or eighth-note.
♪ , or	♪	Semiquaver, or sixteenth-note.
♪ , or	♪	Demi-semiquaver, or thirty-second note.
♪ , or	♪	Semi-demi-semiquaver, or sixty-fourth note.

3.—Each of the above notes in order is, in duration, half the value of the preceding; in Germany and America it is customary to describe each note according to its numerical value (whole-note, half-note, etc.), a plan that has much to recommend it; in England, however, the terms semibreve, minim, etc., are generally used.

4.—The values of the various notes in relation to one another will be clearly seen by the following example:—

Sixty-four	Thirty-two	Sixteen	Eight	Four	Two
= Thirty-two	= Sixteen	= Eight	= Four	= Two	= One
= Sixteen	= Eight	= Four	= Two	= One	
= Eight	= Four	= Two	= One		
= Four	= Two	= One			
= Two	= One				
One					

It must be carefully borne in mind that the above notes represent merely the *relative* duration of sounds, the *actual* duration of any particular note depending upon the speed at which the music is to be played or sung. In this way a semibreve or minim in a quick movement might very well occupy less time than a crotchet or quaver in a slow one, and so on.

5.—It is immaterial whether the stems of minims, crotchets, quavers, etc., be turned up or down; although this is frequently regulated, for appearance sake, by their position on the Staff (Chap. II, Sec. I.)

6.—When two or more quavers, semiquavers, etc., occur in succession, it is usual for them to be grouped together on one tail, thus:—

Such groupings are inseparably connected with the question of Time, and will be fully considered later. (Chap. V.)

7.—The duration of any note may be increased by adding one or more dots after it; a single dot augmenting its value by one-half, e.g.:—

$$\text{♩.} = \text{♩} + \text{♩} = \text{3 crotchets.}$$

$$\text{♩.} = \text{♩} + \text{♪} = \text{3 quavers, etc.}$$

and two dots, by three-quarters, e.g.:—

$$\text{♩..} = \text{♩} + \text{♩} + \text{♪} = \text{7 quavers.}$$

$$\text{♩..} = \text{♩} + \text{♪} + \text{♬} = \text{7 semiquavers, etc.}$$

Carefully observe that the second dot adds half the value of the first dot, i.e., a quarter of the original note. The following rule will be of assistance:—

"A dot always takes half the value of whatever immediately precedes it, whether note or dot."

It will be seen that, whatever number of dots were to be placed after a note, the sum of such dots could never equal the value of the original note.

8.—Sound frequently ceases during the course of a musical composition, and there is silence for a definite period. Such silences are indicated by signs called Rests, corresponding in duration to the notes whose names they take, e.g.:—

Semibreve rest.	Minim rest.	Crotchet rest.	Quaver rest.

Semiquaver rest.	Demi-semiquaver rest.	Semi-demi-semiquaver rest.

9.—Dots are sometimes placed after rests, and increase their duration in the same manner as in the case of notes, e.g.:—

CHAPTER II

PITCH OF SOUNDS—THE STAFF, AND CLEFS

1.—The relative pitch of sounds is expressed by the staff or stave, a species of ladder consisting of a set of parallel lines and the spaces between them. The higher the position of the notes written upon this ladder, the higher (or acuter) will be their pitch; and, vice versa, the lower their position, the lower (or graver) their pitch.

2.—A staff that will include the combined compass of male and female voices is called the Great Staff, and consists of 11 lines and the spaces above and below them:—

The thick line represents "Middle C"—the note nearest the middle of the Pianoforte Keyboard.

3.—Starting from "Middle C," the sounds in alphabetical succession upwards are:—

1st space above "Middle C"	..	..	..	..	..	D.
1st line	,,	,,	..	..	..	.. E.
2nd space	,,	,,	..	..	..	.. F.
2nd line	,,	,,	..	..	..	.. G.
3rd space	,,	,,	..	..	..	.. A.
3rd line	,,	,,	..	..	..	.. B.
4th space	,,	,,	..	..	..	.. C.
4th line	,,	,,	..	..	..	.. D.
5th space	,,	,,	..	..	..	.. E.
5th line	,,	,,	..	..	..	.. F.
6th space	,,	,,	..	..	..	.. G.

Similarly, below "Middle C," the sounds occur alphabetically as under:—

1st space below "Middle C"	..	..	..	..	..	B.
1st line	,,	,,	..	..	..	.. A.
2nd space	,,	,,	..	..	..	.. G.
2nd line	,,	,,	..	..	..	.. F.
3rd space	,,	,,	..	..	..	.. E.
3rd line	,,	,,	..	..	..	.. D.
4th space	,,	,,	..	..	..	.. C.
4th line	,,	,,	..	..	..	.. B.
5th space	,,	,,	..	..	..	.. A.
5th line	,,	,,	..	..	..	.. G.
6th space	,,	,,	..	..	..	.. F.

The following example will show the range of sounds, in alphabetical order, comprised within the limits of the "Great Staff."

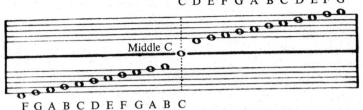

4.—It will be seen, on reference to the above example, that the same letter-name occurs more than once, at a different pitch. Each repetition of a given letter at a higher pitch will produce what is termed the Octave above; and, similarly, each repetition at a lower pitch will produce the Octave below; and it is worthy of note that any two sounds an octave apart have so strong a resemblance to one another (although so distant in actual pitch), that they produce in the mind almost the effect of one sound.

The number of vibrations in any sound is always twice that of the corresponding sound an octave below it.

5.—A staff of eleven lines, such as the above, would not only be found very inconvenient to read from, but the entire compass of any single human voice can be comprised within the limits of far fewer lines and spaces. Hence a selection of a different set for each separate voice is made, as shown in the following diagram by the thick lines:—

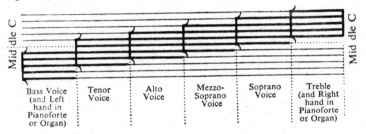

6.—A short staff is thus formed in each instance, consisting of five lines and the spaces above and below them, and representing one of the above sets, thus:—

7.—It will now have been seen that the staff is used to indicate the relative pitch of the various notes placed upon it; but to represent the absolute, definite height or depth of any sound we need certain signs called clefs (Fr. "clef," a key). These show which set of five lines is to be used, and so localise the actual position of the sounds; and, until one of these clefs is placed at the beginning of such a staff, the notes written thereon can bear no names, neither can we know what

sounds they represent. For instance, the note

might represent any one of the following sounds, viz.: C of the Bass voice, G of the Tenor, B of the Alto, D of the Mezzo-Soprano, F of the Soprano, or

A of the Treble (right hand in Pianoforte playing), as will be seen on reference to the diagram in Sec. 5.

8.—Clefs are of three kinds, viz.:—

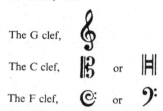

The G clef,

The C clef,   or

The F clef,   or

The C clef is placed on the staff in such a position as always to indicate "Middle C"; the F clef is placed upon the F below that note, and the G clef upon the G above it.

Referring again to the example in Sec. 5, the staves and clefs employed for the various voices, &c. there indicated will appear as under:—

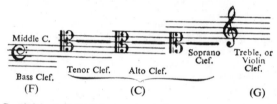

Middle C.

Bass Clef.
(F)   Tenor Clef.   Alto Clef.
(C)   Soprano Clef.   Treble, or Violin Clef.
(G)

The C clef is described in some text-books as a "moveable" clef. The inaccuracy of this statement is shown at a glance by the above diagram, where it will be seen that the clef in reality remains always in the same place, viz., on the line representing "Middle C", the staff in each case being formed by the addition of a greater or less number of lines above or below, as the case may be.

9.—When a staff is formed with the five highest, or five lowest, lines of the Great Staff the note 'Middle C" is not included; consequently the C clef cannot be used, and the two other clefs, viz.: the F and G, are brought into requisition.

These are the clefs most often seen at the present day, and are the only ones now used in Pianoforte, Harp, or Organ music.

The sounds indicated upon the two staves controlled by the F and G clefs are as follows:—

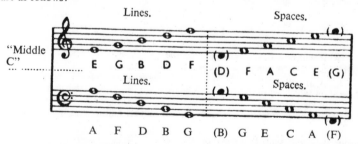

"Middle C"

Lines.   Spaces.

E G B D F   (D) F A C E (G)
Lines.   Spaces.

A F D B G   (B) G E C A (F)

10.—The line for "Middle C" being omitted, this note, when required, is written upon a short line called a Ledger line (Fr. leger, light), the same distance below the Treble staff as it is above the Bass, e.g.:—

Other sounds above and below the pitch of those on the staff are indicated by similar ledger lines, and the spaces between them, e.g.:—

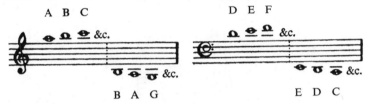

11.—The C clef was formely more frequently used than at the present time. Nowadays, its employment is confined to certain orchestral instruments, and occasionally (particularly in foreign scores) to the Soprano, Alto and Tenor voices. The following table will show the method of its use:—

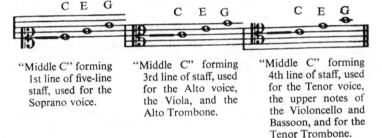

"Middle C" forming 1st line of five-line staff, used for the Soprano voice.

"Middle C" forming 3rd line of staff, used for the Alto voice, the Viola, and the Alto Trombone.

"Middle C" forming 4th line of staff, used for the Tenor voice, the upper notes of the Violoncello and Bassoon, and for the Tenor Trombone.

The fallacy of describing the C clef as a moveable one is again shown in this example.

In England and America, the vocal parts are nearly always written in the F and G clefs; but a distinct advantage of the use of the C clef is that practically the whole compass of any particular voice is included on the staff, without the use of ledger-lines. When the G clef is used (as it commonly is) for the Tenor voice, the notes are written an octave higher than they sound, a plan tending to obscure their true pitch in the mind of the performer, e.g.:—

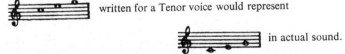

12.—It will be observed that the three notes written above are in each case identical in pitch; they could be represented in the G and F clefs respectively, thus:—

13.—In music for the Pianoforte, Harp, or Organ, the two staves are usually connected by a sign called a Brace, thus:—

and, unless specially indicated otherwise, the notes in the Treble, or G clef, are played with the right hand, and those in the Bass, or F clef, with the left hand.

CHAPTER III

SHARPS, FLATS, AND NATURALS

1.—A chain of sounds such as that given in Chapter II, Sec. 3, although an alphabetical one, is not one in which the distances between the successive notes are in all cases equal, the difference in pitch between the notes B—C and E—F being smaller than that between any other two notes in alphabetical order.

2.—It will be observed that, on the Pianoforte or Organ keyboard, there are in two instances two white keys next to one another, without a black key between; but that, in all other cases, a black key separates two succeeding white ones thus:—

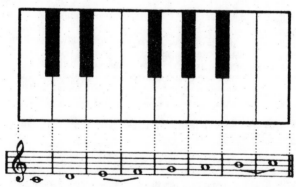

(Sounds represented by the white keys in order, starting
from "Middle C.")

3.—In the above diagram, the distance from one white key to another, when no black key comes between, is called a semitone—being found between E and F, and between B and C, a whole tone occurring between any other successive white keys. The semitone is the smallest distance from one note to another on the Pianoforte or Organ keyboard. Voices, and instruments of the "String" family, such as the Violin, Viola, Violoncello, &c., can produce sounds whose distance from one another is smaller than a semitone; but, for most practical purposes, the semitone is regarded as the smallest.

4.—The black keys represent the sounds lying at the distance of a semitone above or below the adjacent white keys, and are termed sharps and flats.

5.—A sharp, ♯, placed before a note raises the pitch of that note one semitone, and a flat, ♭, lowers it one semitone. By the following diagram it will be seen that, in this way, each black key may represent a sharp or a flat; a chain of semitones resulting in each case:—

(Read this line from left to right.)

(Read this line from right to left.)

begin here.

When the two notes of a semitone are expressed by the same letter-name, as C to C♯, or C to C♭, the semitone is termed chromatic; when they are expressed by two different letters, as C to D♭, or C to B, it is called diatonic.

6.—When a sharp or a flat is placed immediately after the clef, it is intended that all the notes of the same name, occurring during the entire composition (or section of the same) are to be similarly sharpened or flattened, unless the contrary is indicated (see Sec. 7); e.g.:—

signifies that all F's and C's are to be sharp.

signifies that all B's, E's and A's are to be flat.

The **signs** so placed at the beginning of the staff constitute what is known as the Key-signature. (Chap. VI, Sec. 8.)

7.—Oftentimes it is necessary temporarily to sharpen or flatten a note; in this case, the sharp or flat is placed immediately before the note and is termed an Accidental:—

(a) described as "G sharp."   *(b)* described as "G flat."

When it is desired to restore such note to its normal pitch a sign called a Natural, ♮, is placed before it:-

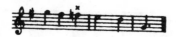

described as "G" natural.

This is called contradicting the accidental. In cases where the key-signature contains one or more sharps or flats, it is evident that the natural itself may become an accidental; e.g.:—

It will be seen that, after a ♯ has been used, a ♮ lowers the pitch of the note a semitone again; and similarly raises it, after a ♭ has been used.

8.—Double-sharps and double-flats are frequently met with as accidentals. A double-sharp, X, has the effect of raising an already sharpened note a semitone —i.e., a whole tone above the "natural" pitch; and a double-flat, ♭♭, similarly lowers an already flattened note a semitone—i.e., a whole tone below the "natural" pitch, e.g.:—

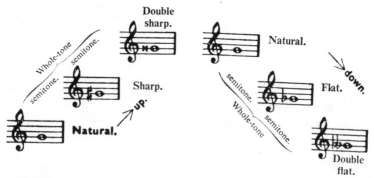

9.—Unfortunately, there are two methods of contradicting double-sharps, or double-flats. In order to lower a double-sharp by a semitone to a single sharp, some composers write—

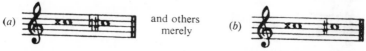

(a)   and others merely   *(b)*

and in order to raise a double-flat, similarly, to a single flat, both of the following methods are used:—

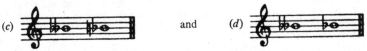

The plan adopted at (*b*) and (*d*) is to be recommended as being simpler and less cumbersome.

10.—Accidentals, of whatever kind, affect all notes of the same pitch throughout an entire bar, or measure (see Chap. IV, Sec. 3), unless contradicted, but no further. If an accidental is to apply to notes of the same letter-name, but in a different octave, it should be indicated again in that particular position, e.g.:—

&c.

11.—When the last note of a bar, or measure, has been inflected by an accidental, and the next bar begins with a note of the same letter-name, restored to its original pitch, it is safer specially to indicate the change, e.g.:—

although, if the rule in Sec 10 were always acted upon by composers this would not be necessary.

12.—In connection with the subject of sharps and flats, it is worth while to note that each pianoforte key, except the black key lying between G and A, may be called by three names, e.g.:—C = B♯ = D♭♭, F♯ = G♭ = EX, and so on. The black key above referred to can bear only two names, viz.: G♯ and A♭.

———

CHAPTER IV

ACCENT AND TIME

1.—To produce a satisfactory musical effect, it is not only necessary that there should be (i) variety of pitch, and (ii) duration of sound, but also (iii) what is termed Accent. The grouping of sounds into sets by means of accent produces what is known as Time, not to be confused with Tempo, which means the speed at which a composition is to be played or sung.

2.—In a well-ordered succession of sounds, producing what is commonly called a Melody, or Tune, it cannot have escaped the student's notice that certain of these sounds are accented more strongly than others; and that, periodically, there is a recurrence of an accent stronger than the rest, which, for the sake of convenience, we will call the Strongest Accent, e.g.:—

3.—To indicate the position of this constantly recurring Strongest Accent, it is nowadays customary to place a perpendicular line—from top to bottom of the staff—immediately before such accent. The above passage would thus appear as follows:—

Such lines are termed Bar-lines, and as much as is contained between any two successive bar-lines is described as a Measure or a Bar of music. At the conclusion of a composition, or sometimes at the termination of a period, or musical sentence, two somewhat thicker lines are drawn, called a Double-bar, e.g.:—

These, however, do not always mark the situation of the accent,

neither do they affect the time (as in the following example):—

The double-bars here merely indicate the end of a line of words in the hymn to which the tune is set, and the time is not broken at X.

4.—The Strongest Accent in musical passages may recur at a greater or less distance of time, producing as a consequence, bars of various lengths—bars in which there are, as the case may be, two, three, or four divisions, pulses, or beats (as they are usually called, from the practice of "beating" time). Bars with five, or seven such divisions are sometimes met with.

5.—The kinds of Time produced—depending, be it observed, entirely upon this periodic recurrence of the Strongest Accent—may be classified under three headings, viz.:—

Duple (in which each bar is divisible into two beats of equal value), e.g.:—

Triple (in which each bar is divisible into three such beats), e.g.:—

Quadruple (in which each bar is divisible into four such beats), e.g.:—

Quadruple time being practically an extension of Duple time, an accent will occur on the third beat, but it will be slighter than that on the first beat.

6.—As it is usual for one kind of Time to be maintained for a considerable portion of a composition—often for the whole of it—it is customary to indicate, at the beginning of the piece, the particular kind of Time in which it is written. For this purpose a sign called a Time-Signature is used, which (except in two instances) consists of two figures, an upper and a lower, thus:—

$$\frac{2}{4} \qquad\qquad \frac{3}{8} \qquad\qquad \frac{4}{16} \,\&c.$$

the upper figure showing the number of divisions in a bar, and the lower specifying their quality, or value.

7.—In order to indicate the value of the beats or divisions, whether minims crotchets, quavers, semiquavers, &c., the lower figure is always an aliquot part of a semibreve (which note is taken as the standard from which the others are reckoned), e.g.:—

$$\overline{2} \qquad\qquad \overline{4} \qquad\qquad \overline{8} \qquad\qquad \overline{16} \;\&c.$$

8.—When each beat of a bar is divisible by two (i.e., when it can be represented by two of the notes next smaller in value), the time is called Simple. Thus we have Simple Duple Time, Simple Triple Time, and Simple Quadruple Time, the more usual time-signatures being:—

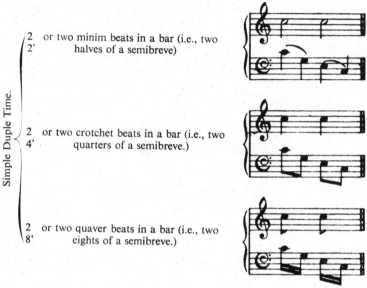

Simple Duple Time.

2 or two minim beats in a bar (i.e., two
2' halves of a semibreve)

2 or two crotchet beats in a bar (i.e., two
4' quarters of a semibreve.)

2 or two quaver beats in a bar (i.e., two
8' eights of a semibreve.)

Simple Triple Time.

3 or three minim beats in a bar.
2'

3 or three crotchet beats in a bar.
4'

3 or three quaver beats in a bar.
8'

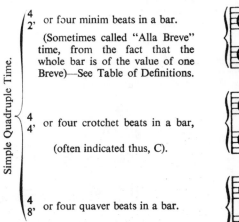

Simple Quadruple Time.

$\frac{4}{2}$, or four minim beats in a bar.

(Sometimes called "Alla Breve" time, from the fact that the whole bar is of the value of one Breve)—See Table of Definitions.

$\frac{4}{4}$, or four crotchet beats in a bar,

(often indicated thus, C).

$\frac{4}{8}$, or four quaver beats in a bar.

It is very rarely that we find times in which the beats are of the value of semibreves or notes shorter than quavers. There are, however, two rather well-known instances of

$\frac{3}{1}$ (three semibreves in a bar) in Clementi's "Gradus ad Parnassum."

9.—Oftentimes the character of the music requires each beat of a bar to be divisible by three (i.e., represented by a triplet—see Table of Definitions) of the notes next smaller in value, e.g.:—

To save the necessity of marking the triplets throughout an entire composition of this kind, a new time-signature is employed, in which the lower figure indicates the quality of each note of the triplet—as an aliquot part of a semibreve. Thus, the above passage would appear as follows:—

Here the signature means that six eighths of a semibreve (viz., six quavers) are to be taken in each bar, divided into groups of three, each group constituting one

beat, and being consequently of the value of a dotted crotchet. Hence the above time would be described as having two dotted crotchet-beats in a bar. Observe that the dotted beats in the second of the above examples are of exactly the same duration as the undotted beats in the first.

10.—When the beats of a bar are dotted, the time is termed compound, and thus we have Compound Duple time, Compound Triple time, and Compound Quadruple time, the more usual time-signatures then being—

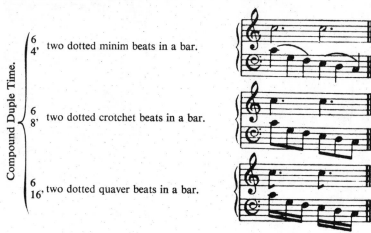

Compound Duple Time.

$\frac{6}{4}$, two dotted minim beats in a bar.

$\frac{6}{8}$, two dotted crotchet beats in a bar.

$\frac{6}{16}$, two dotted quaver beats in a bar.

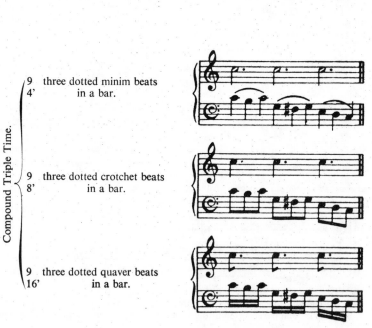

Compound Triple Time.

$\frac{9}{4}$, three dotted minim beats in a bar.

$\frac{9}{8}$, three dotted crotchet beats in a bar.

$\frac{9}{16}$, three dotted quaver beats in a bar.

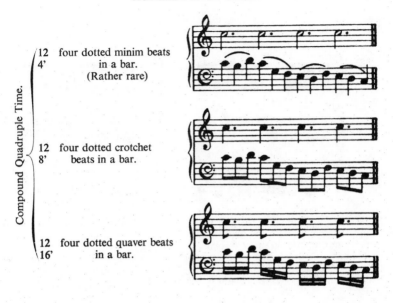

Compound Quadruple Time.

| $\frac{12}{4}$ | four dotted minim beats in a bar. (Rather rare) |

| $\frac{12}{8}$ | four dotted crotchet beats in a bar. |

| $\frac{12}{16}$ | four dotted quaver beats in a bar. |

11.—It will be readily understood from the examples in Secs. 8 and 10, that the divisions or beats of a bar may always be expressed by their equivalent value in notes of shorter or longer duration, or by an equivalent number of notes and rests, e.g.:—

(a) (b)

(c) (d)

(e) (f) &c.

CHAPTER V

THE GROUPING OF NOTES

1.—When the divisions of a bar are represented by their equivalent value in quavers, semiquavers, &c., it is the custom for these notes to be grouped together. In vocal music, only as many notes may be grouped together as are sung to one syllable. Such groupings should always indicate, as far as possible, the divisions, or beats, in order to make their position clear to the eye. Thus, it may be taken as a safe rule that only as many notes should be grouped together as would form one beat, but that the notes belonging to each beat should be so grouped, e.g.:—

Examples of this rule could easily be multiplied, but the above instances, both of its observance and of its non-observance, will be sufficient to show the necessity of correct groupings, in order to make clear the equal divisions of the bar. It should be borne in mind, in connection with the question of the sub-division of the beats of a bar, that the first note of any such sub-division is always stronger than the remaining ones, and that it thus forms a subordinate accent, e.g.:—

Here the main accent of course occurs at the beginning of the first beat; but the F and G (the first note of the second and third beats respectively) are more strongly emphasised than the other notes of their own groups. This rule applies in a similar way to every further sub-division into groups of shorter notes.

2.—Exceptions to the rule given in Sec. 1, occur as under:—

(i) In the case of $\frac{4}{4}$ time, when it is customary to group quavers in fours, where a clear half-bar is indicated by each four, e.g.:—

(ii.) In the case of $\frac{3}{4}$ or $\frac{3}{8}$ time, when it is usual to arrange the six quavers of $\frac{3}{4}$, or the six semiquavers of $\frac{3}{8}$, in one group, e.g.:—

3.—In the matter of the employment of rests, no rest of greater value than one beat should be used (except in two instances mentioned in Sec. 4), e.g.:—

4.—There are two exceptions to this rule, viz.:—

(i.) In the case of a whole bar's rest, when a semibreve rest is used in all times, save the true "Alla Breve" $\left(\text{or } \frac{4}{2}\right)$ time, when a breve rest is used, appropriately:—

(ii.) In the case of a clear half-bar at either end of a bar of quadruple time, when a rest of the value of that half-bar should be used:—

5.—With regard to notes, a greater freedom is permissible, and a sound lasting during more than one beat is often represented by a single note, e.g.:—

Observe, however, that in compound times, this can only occur when the sound lasts for two or more whole beats:—

Good.

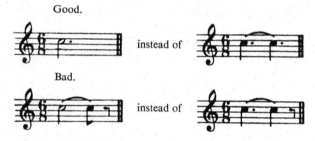

Bad.

6.—When a bar has to be completed with rests, care must be taken that each beat (or sub-division of the same) must be finished before the next is begun. The following example will illustrate this:—

Good.

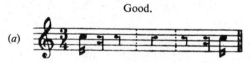

(a)

Here, in $\frac{3}{4}$ time, each beat consists of a crotchet. The note at the beginning of the bar has taken a quarter of the first beat; therefore, a semiquaver rest must succeed, to fill up the first half; a quaver rest following, by which the entire beat is completed. The second beat of the bar is intact, consequently a crotchet rest is used. In the case of the third beat the semiquaver note at the end of the bar represents the last quarter of that beat, which will be completed in the same manner as in the case of the first part of the bar—only in the reverse order.

Bad.

(b)

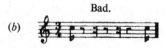

This example, although it contains the same rests as the bar at (a), is totally incorrect, as their order gives no idea of the position of the various divisions, or sub-divisions.

7.—If $\frac{6}{8}$ (compound duple) were to be substituted for $\frac{3}{4}$ in Ex. (*a*), the order of rests would be as follows:—

Here each beat is of the value of a dotted note, as shown by the small notes above the example, and it should be remembered that in the case of compound times, the value of each of such notes—without its dot—should always be completed with rests first, a separate rest being used for the dot. Hence, in the above example, the first ⌐rotchet having been broken into, is completed by the addition of, first, a semiquaver rest, and then a quaver rest (see Sec. 6)—a second quaver rest then succeeding, as the equivalent of the dot.

In the second half-bar, the case is different. The semiquaver note at the end of the bar has taken the latter half of the dot, and consequently needs a semiquaver rest before it, to fill up the value of that dot. A crotchet rest (not two quaver rests) then precedes, to represent the unbroken crotchet at the beginning of the second beat.

8.—Syncopation is an effect in music caused by throwing additional emphasis upon what is usually a weaker part of a bar. The most common instances of this are found when a note is begun

      (i.) On a comparatively unaccented part of a bar, and prolonged into
           the next accent, as at (*a*); or
      (ii.) In the midst of one beat, and prolonged into the next, as at (*b*).

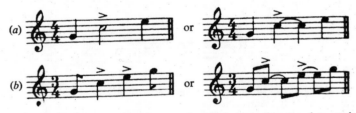

The effect of syncopation is, moreover, produced whenever the natural accent is disturbed by any means—by ties, rests, etc., e.g.:—

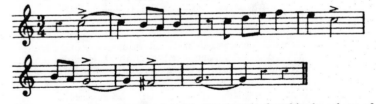

A strong instance of syncopation in triple time is to be found in the *scherzo* of Beethoven's "Eroica" symphony, where the following passage occurs:—

CHAPTER VI

THE MAJOR SCALE

1.—A scale (L. scala, a ladder) is a stepwise succession of sounds, having reference to one particular sound as its starting-point, or key-note.

2.—As was stated in Chap. II. Sec. 2, the first seven letters of the alphabet are employed to express the different sounds in use. The re-appearance of the same letter at a different pitch produces what is known as the octave of the sound originally indicated by that letter, thus:—

A continuation, alphabetically, of this series, higher or lower, would be merely a reproduction of these sounds at a higher or lower pitch—in other words, in a higher or lower octave.

3.—If the student will play the succession of notes in Sec. 2 on the Pianoforte (represented by the white keys), he will find that the distances between the notes are not in all cases equal.

For instance, the first four notes contain two steps of a tone each, and one of a semitone, thus:—

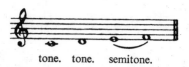

tone.   tone.   semitone.

Proceeding further, it will be seen that the remaining four sounds of the octave are on exactly the same pattern:—

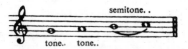

Each of these groups of four notes alphabetically arranged is called a **tetrachord** (Gr. τέτρα, four; χορδή, a string), and together form what is termed the Major Diatonic scale (Gr. διὰ, through; τόνος, a tone, i.e., through the tones, or sounds).

(Scale of C major)

4.—This Major Scale—i.e., a scale having a semitone between its 3rd and 4th degrees, and also between its 7th and 8th degrees—may not only begin upon C as its key-note, or starting point, but may be reproduced at a different pitch, any one of the seven letters above-mentioned being taken as the key-note, and also the sharpened and flattened forms of these letters.

Clearly, however, the white keys of the Pianoforte, or natural notes, would not suffice for the purpose, as were they only to be used, the above order of tones and semitones would not be preserved, e.g.:—

Hence, we must employ the black keys, representing certain sharps and flats, e.g.:—

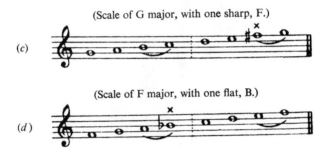

(Scale of G major, with one sharp, F.)

(Scale of F major, with one flat, B.)

by which the tones and semitones are brought into their right positions.

5.—It will be seen, by Ex. (c) above, that the first tetrachord of the scale of G major corresponds to the second tetrachord of C major, and that the scale of G is completed by adding a new tetrachord, containing a sharpened note (the seventh of the entire scale).

Similarly, if we take the second tetrachord of this scale (G) as the first tetrachord of a new scale, and then add another tetrachord, we shall find it necessary again to sharpen the note before the last, in order to preserve the order of tones and semitones:—

(Scale of D major, with two sharps, F and C.)

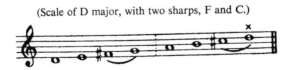

6.—It will thus be found that a series of major scales can be formed, each succeeding scale beginning on the 5th note of the preceding, and having one sharp more, the extra sharp being always the 7th degree (or Leading-note—see Sec. 9) of the entire scale. The following diagram will show this at a glance:—

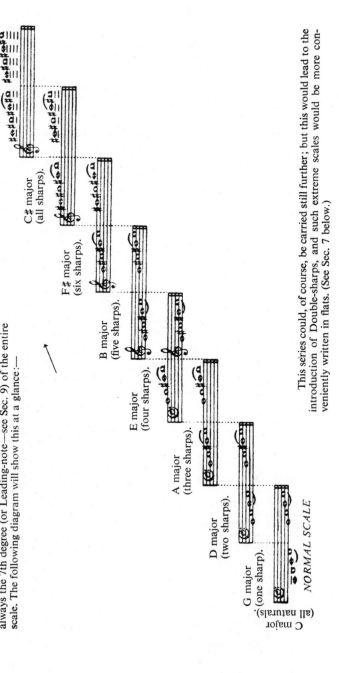

C major (all naturals).

G major (one sharp).

NORMAL SCALE

D major (two sharps).

A major (three sharps).

E major (four sharps).

B major (five sharps).

F♯ major (six sharps).

C♯ major (all sharps).

This series could, of course, be carried still further; but this would lead to the introduction of Double-sharps, and such extreme scales would be more conveniently written in flats. (See Sec. 7 below.)

7.—Similarly, a series of major scales with flats can be formed—(each succeeding scale beginning on the 4th degree of the preceding, i.e., five notes lower)—the extra flat always being the 4th degree of the new scale thus produced:—

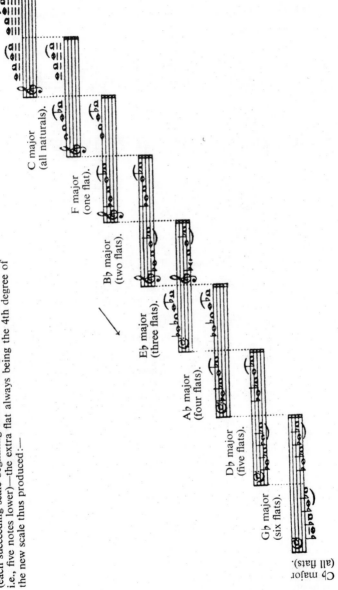

NORMAL SCALE.

C major (all naturals).

F major (one flat).

Bb major (two flats).

Eb major (three flats).

Ab major (four flats).

Db major (five flats).

Gb major (six flats).

Cb major (all flats).

8.—To save unnecessary complication in writing, the sharps and flats in such scales are placed at the beginning of a musical composition, immediately after the clef. They then form what is known as the key-signature. (Chap. III, Sec. 6.)

The key-signatures of the above two series of scales would appear as under:—

(*a*) Scales with sharps.

(*b*) Scales with flats.

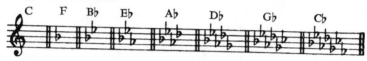

It should be observed that these sharps and flats must be placed in the signature in regular order, as developed from the natural scale according to the plan mentioned in Secs. 6 and 7 above.

9.—Every degree of a (major or minor) diatonic scale has a technical name, as follows:—

1st degree	Tonic, or Key-note	..	The note from which the whole scale, key, or tonality springs.
2nd ,,	Super-tonic	.. ..	The note next above the Tonic.
3rd ,,	Mediant	.. ..	The note midway between the Tonic and the Dominant.
4th ,,	Sub-dominant	..	Under-dominant, holding same position under the Tonic as the Dominant does above it.
5th ,,	Dominant	.. ..	The note next in importance to the Tonic, having a dominating influence over the key.
6th ,,	Sub-mediant	.. ..	Under-mediant, the note holding the same position below the Tonic, midway between it and the Sub-dominant, as the Mediant does above the Tonic, midway between it and the Dominant.
7th ,,	Leading-note	.. ..	The note that leads the ear to expect the Tonic, or Key-note.

CHAPTER VII

THE MINOR SCALE

1.—The Minor scale derives its name from the fact that its 3rd degree is a chromatic semitone lower than the corresponding degree of the major scale, consequently producing a smaller (or minor) interval from the Tonic to the Mediant, e.g. :—

(In C major).   (In C minor.)

2.—The Minor scale exists in more than one form; in each of which, however, the first tetrachord is the same, e.g.:—

(C minor.)

the semitone occurring between the 2nd and 3rd degrees, instead of between the 3rd and 4th, as in the Major scale.

3.—The second tetrachord may be found in either of the following forms:—

It will be seen that No. i. has the step of a semitone between the 7th and 8th degrees. No. iii. between the 5th and 6th; whereas No. ii. has semitones both between the 5th and 6th, and the 7th and 8th degrees.

4.—The most usual form nowadays is that termed the Harmonic Minor Scale, in which the second tetrachord is that given as No. ii. above:—

3 semi-
tones.

This scale is termed Harmonic, as it is the one from which the harmonies of a minor key are most usually formed.

5.—The tetrachords given as Nos. i. and iii. in Sec. 3 are rarely found except as the ascending and descending forms, respectively, of the scale known as the Melodic Minor Scale:—

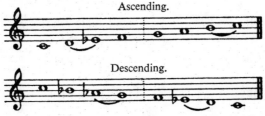

Ascending.

Descending.

a scale used by composers at times to avoid the somewhat hard effect in melody of the step of a tone-and-a-half between the 6th and 7th degrees of the Harmonic Minor Scale.

It should be noticed that, in the Melodic Minor Scale, as shown above, the Tonic is approached by step of a semitone, ascending; and the Dominant by a similar step, descending.

6.—The method of writing the signature of a Minor scale is a singularly unfortunate one, representing neither of the above forms accurately. The plan is to make the signature of a minor scale coincide with that of the major scale that begins on its 3rd degree, e.g.:—

> A minor has the same signature as C major
>
> E minor has the same signature as G major

and so on.

These scales, having the same signature, are termed relative major and minor scales.

7.—Returning for a moment to the harmonic scale of C minor given in Sec. 4 above, and applying this rule, it will be found that its signature is that of the scale of E♭ major (its 3rd degree), thus:—

the Leading-note being written with an accidental to cause the semitone to occur between the 7th and 8th degrees.

Here the anomalous character of the signature will be seen, for a B♭ appears therein, only to be contradicted when we arrive at the Leading-note of the scale.

When the Melodic Minor Scale is considered, the matter is no better, as A♮ is required in ascending, and the signature contains A♭.

8.—The signatures of the various minor keys are therefore as follows:—

A MINOR,	with same signature as	C MAJOR,
	1.—Sharp keys.	
E MINOR,	with same signature as	G MAJOR,
B MINOR,	,,	,,	D MAJOR,
F♯ MINOR,	,,	,,	A MAJOR,
C♯ MINOR,	,,	,,	E MAJOR,
G♯ MINOR,	,,	,,	B MAJOR,
D♯ MINOR	,,	,,	F♯ MAJOR,
A♯ MINOR,	,,	,,	C♯ MAJOR,

A MINOR,	with same signature as	C MAJOR,	
	2.—Flat keys.		
D MINOR,	with same signature as	F MAJOR	
G MINOR,	,,	,,	Bb MAJOR,
C MINOR,	,,	,,	Eb MAJOR,
F MINOR,	,,	,,	Ab MAJOR
Bb MINOR,	,,	,,	Db MAJOR,
Eb MINOR,	,,	,,	Gb MAJOR
Ab MINOR,	,,	,,	Cb MAJOR,

9.—A major and a minor scale starting from the same tonic, or keynote, are termed respectively the Tonic Major, or Tonic Minor, of each other:—

    (i.) C major   :   Tonic minor = C minor.
    (ii.) C major   :   Tonic major = C major.

It will be seen from the diagram in Sec. 8 that there is always a difference of three signs between the signatures of a major scale and its Tonic minor.

CHAPTER VIII

THE CHROMATIC SCALE

1.—A Chromatic Scale (Gr $\chi\acute{\omega}\rho\mu\alpha$, colour), is a scale proceeding entirely by semitones, the number of sounds between any note and its octave being twelve, e.g. :—

2.—The student will observe that all the Pianoforte keys, black as well as white, are needed to form this scale.

3.—The Chromatic scale is found written in more ways than one, that given in Sec. 1 being termed the Harmonic Chromatic Scale, from the fact that the chromatic harmonies of any key need this particular notation for their proper formation.

4.—The Harmonic Chromatic Scale is constructed as follows, and each key has its own chromatic scale, formed upon exactly the same plan:—

(a) Take the notes of the Major diatonic scale of the particular key in question—e.g. (in key of C):—

(b) Add the notes that differ from these in both forms of the Minor diatonic scale:—

In Harmonic Minor.

In Melodic Minor (descending form).

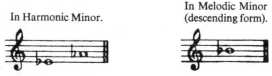

We now have the following:—

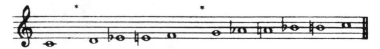

with gaps as yet between the Tonic and Supertonic, and between the Sub-dominant and Dominant. To complete the Chromatic Scale, we must finally add the diatonic semitone above the key-note, and the chromatic semitone above the sub-dominant. The following examples will make this clear:—

In key of C.

In key of B♭.

In key of E.

5.—The above is the chromatic scale, formed upon a harmonic basis, but it is often found modified in notation, for the purpose of lessening the number of accidentals, and so simplifying matters for the reader of music. These alterations are purely for convenience, however, and vary from time to time, according to the circumstances in which they are needed, the most usual form of Arbitrary (or Melodic) Chromatic Scale—as it is generally termed—being the following:—

(or B♭)

6.—It will be seen, by comparing this form of scale with that given in Sec. 4, that, in ascending, the number of accidentals is much reduced, the scales remaining, however, identical in notation in the descending form.

7.—From this we may form the rules that are generally observed in writing the Arbitrary Chromatic Scale, viz.:—

(i.) That the notes that are diatonic in the particular key are always kept unaltered;

(ii.) That the raised Sub-dominant is always used, ascending or descending, in preference to the lowered Dominant, as being more closely related to the key;

(iii.) That the remaining notes are formed by raising existing ones a chromatic semitone in ascending, and by lowering them a semitone in descending.

The same letter-name must never occur more than twice in succession.
The following examples will illustrate these rules:—

(Key of E♭ ; Major mode.)

(Key of E♭ ; Minor mode.)   (a) (b)

(a) Diatonic in descending Melodic Minor form.   (Chap. VII, Sec. 5.)
(b) Really a diatonic note in the key, although written with an accidental.   (Chap. VII, Sec. 7.)

The notes corresponding to Rule (i.) are printed as open notes.
The note corresponding to Rule (ii.) is printed as an open note enclosed in brackets.
The notes corresponding to Rule (iii.) are printed as black-headed notes.

CHAPTER IX

INTERVALS

1.—An Interval is the difference in pitch between two sounds

2.—Intervals are described numerically, and are so reckoned from the number of letter-names included in their formation, e g.:—

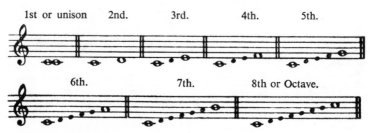

Here it will be seen that the 1st, or unison, contains only one letter-name; a 2nd, two; a 3rd, three, and so on.

3 —The inflection of either note of an interval—or of both—by an accidental does not alter its numerical description; but, as will be seen later, it causes its quality to be varied.

Thus, each of the following comes under the description of a 3rd, as between C and E there is only one letter-name, D:—

4.—The quality of an interval depends upon the number of semitones contained therein. For instance, Exs. (i.), (vi.), and (vii.) contain four semitones each; Exs. (ii.), (iii), and (viii), three; and Exs (iv.) and (v), two; and, according to the number of semitones they contain, would be described as major, minor, and diminished 3rds, respectively.

5.—The various kinds of interval produced in this way bear the following names:—

	(i.) Perfect	..	(applied only 1sts, 4ths, 5ths, and 8ths.
Imperfect	(ii.) Major	..⎫	(,, ,, 2nds, 3rds, 6ths, and 7ths).
	(iii.) Minor	..⎭	
	(iv.) Diminished..	(	,, ,, 3rds, 4ths, 5ths, and 7ths).
	(v.) Augmented..	(	,, ,, 2nds, 4ths, 5ths, and 6ths).

6.—The intervals counted from the Tonic to any of the notes of a major scale are either major or perfect, e.g.:—

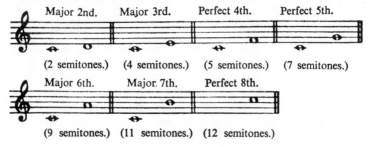

7.—A minor interval is formed by lowering the upper note of a major interval (or by raising its lower note) a chromatic semitone, thus retaining letter-names, e.g.:—

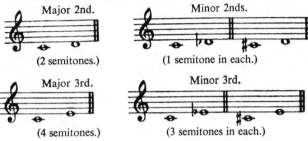

—and similarly with the intervals of 6th and 7th.

8.—A diminished interval is produced by similarly lowering the upper note of a minor, or a perfect interval (or by raising its lower note) a chromatic semitone, e.g.:—

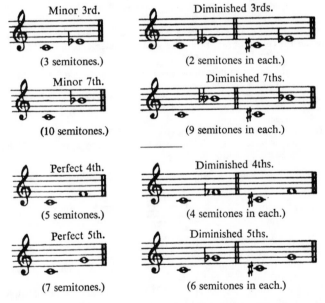

9.—An augmented interval is produced, conversely, by raising the upper note of a major, or a perfect interval (or by lowering its under note) a chromatic semitone, e.g.:—

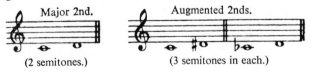

(9 semitones.)   (10 semitones in each.)

The intervals of Diminished 6th and Augmented 3rd are not employed in chord-formation, therefore are not included here, being practically useless.

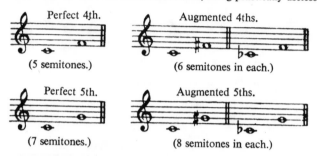

(5 semitones.)   (6 semitones in each.)

(7 semitones.)   (8 semitones in each.)

10.—In order to find the interval between two sounds, it will be of service to remember the rule in Sec. 6. From this, and the statements in Secs. 7, 8 and 9, it is possible to form the following plan:—

(i.) Take the lower note of the given interval, and regard it as if it were the Tonic, or key-note of a major scale.

(ii.) If the upper note corresponds to one of the degrees of the major scale of that Tonic, the interval will, as stated above, be either major or perfect.

(iii.) If the upper note does not so correspond to one of the degrees of that major scale, its quality may easily be found by applying to it the rules in Secs. 7, 8 and 9 above.

The following examples will make this clear. Take the interval:—

Again, take the interval—

Here regard the lower note as the tonic of the scale of D major. The interval is clearly a 3rd, as it contains three letter-names (Sec 2). The interval of 3rd, counted from the tonic, in the major scale of D, is F♯. This is a major 3rd, according to the statement in Sec. 6.

D to F♮ would be a minor 3rd (Sec. 7), and D to F♭ (the interval in question) would be a diminished 3rd (Sec. 8).

Here regard the lower note as the tonic of E major. The interval is a 5th, as it contains five letter-names. The interval of 5th, counted from the tonic, in the major scale of E, is B♮. This is a perfect 5th (Sec. 6); consequently E to B♯ is an augmented 5th (Sec. 9).

11.—An interval is termed—

Consonant, or Concordant, when it is satisfactory in itself, and requires no other to follow it to complete its effect; and

Dissonant, or Discordant, when, on the contrary, it does require another to follow it, to render its effect satisfactory.

In the first class are:

(i.) Major and Minor 3rds and 6ths.

(ii.) All Perfect intervals (except, occasionally, the perfect 4th). (*See* Chap. XIII, Sec. 13,).

In the second are included:

(i.) All 2nds, 7ths, and 9ths.

(ii.) All Diminished and Augmented intervals.

12.—Intervals beyond the limits of an Octave are called Compound Intervals, e.g.:—

13.—The terms Diatonic and Chromatic are also applied to intervals. The former are those which can be found in any diatonic scale; the latter those which occur only in the chromatic scale, viz.:—

(i.) The Chromatic semitone (or augmented 1st).

(ii.) The Diminished 3rd.

(iii.) The Augmented 6th.

(iv.) The Diminished 8th.

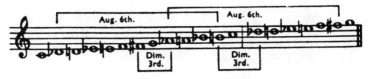

14.—By inverting an interval is meant the changing of the relative position of the two notes, effected by placing the lower note an 8ve higher, or the higher note an 8ve lower, e.g.:—

15.—The number of the original interval added to the number of the inverted interval produces nine:—

A	2nd inverted becomes a 7th			$2 + 7 = 9.$
A	3rd	,,	,, 6th	$3 + 6 = 9.$
A	4th	,,	,, 5th	$4 + 5 = 9.$
A	5th	,,	,, 4th	$5 + 4 = 9.$
A	6th	,,	,, 3rd	$6 + 3 = 9.$
A	7th	,,	,, 2nd	$7 + 2 = 9.$
An	8th	,,	,, 1st	$8 + 1 = 9.$

16.—Further, it should be observed that, when inverted—

  (i.) Major intervals become Minor.
  (ii.) Minor intervals become Major.
  (iii.) Diminished intervals become Augmented.
  (iv.) Augmented intervals become Diminished.

but that—

  (v.) Perfect intervals remain Perfect.

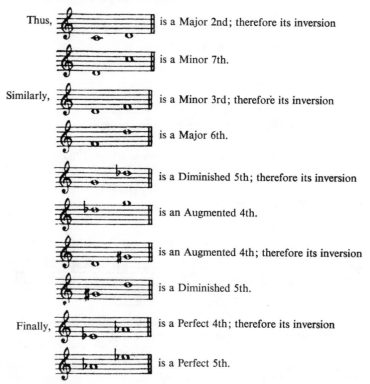

Thus,   is a Major 2nd; therefore its inversion

is a Minor 7th.

Similarly,   is a Minor 3rd; therefore its inversion

is a Major 6th.

is a Diminished 5th; therefore its inversion

is an Augmented 4th.

is an Augmented 4th; therefore its inversion

is a Diminished 5th.

Finally,   is a Perfect 4th; therefore its inversion

is a Perfect 5th.

Instances might be multiplied, but the above will be quite sufficient to show the working of the rules of inversion, as applied to intervals.

17.—The number of semitones contained in any interval added to those contained in its inversion will necessarily produce the number of semitones contained in an 8ve, viz.:—12, e.g.:—

The interval   contains 4 semitones;

Its inversion   contains 8 semitones

4 + 8 = 12 semitones, the number contained in the entire 8ve.

CHAPTER X

SIGNS OF ABBREVIATION AND EMBELLISHMENT

1.—When it is desired that a section of a composition shall be repeated, such repeat is usually indicated by that particular section being marked off, at beginning and end, by double bars, the first of which has two or four dots placed after it, and the second, similar dots placed before it, thus:—

2.—If the repeat is to be made from the beginning of a piece of music, the first double-bar is unnecessary.

3.—When, on the repetition, an alteration of the termination of the passage is needed, this is indicated as under:—

Here, when the repeat is made, the bars marked 2nd time are to be substituted for those marked 1st time.

4.—Sometimes a repeat from the commencement of a piece is indicated by the words Da Capo (i.e., from the beginning), or merely the initials D.C., placed at that point from which the return is to be made.

The term Dal Segno (i.e., from the sign), or merely the initials D.S., similarly direct that such return shall be made to a point marked by this sign ·$. In both these cases the repetition is continued until the word Fine (end) occurs, or until a double bar with a pause mark above it is reached. (See Sec. 6.)

5.—The word bis over a bar, or similar short passage, signifies that such bar or passage is to be performed twice. This sign is rarely met with nowadays, except in MS. music.

6.—The sign ⌒, a Pause, over or under a note or rest has the effect of prolonging its length, the precise amount of such lengthening being left to the discretion of the performer (See, however, Sec. 4.) The words Lunga pausa (a long pause) show that the pause is to be of considerable duration.

The initials G.P. (Grosse, or General, Pause) are sometimes met with in orchestral music, and indicate a pause for the whole band

7.—To avoid the use of an inconvenient number of ledger lines, the extreme high notes above the staff are frequently written thus:—

the sign 8va (or merely 8......), being an abbreviation of the word ottava, and indicating that the sounds over which it and the dots following it are placed are to be played an octave higher. The resumption of the ordinary pitch is indicated by the cessation of the dots, or sometimes by the term loco (in place).

8va bassa (Ottava bassa), or 8va sotto (Ottava sotto), under the bass staff indicates similarly that such notes are to be played an octave lower.

Con 8 (or 8) under a bass-note means that such bass-note is to be accompanied by its Octave below, thus:—

8.—The signs } and (placed before a chord (see App. A), indicate that the notes of that chord are not to be played together, but in arpeggio (Ital. arpa, a harp), i.e., in rapid succession, beginning with the lowest:—

the whole chord being held when all the notes have been sounded.

9.—The term **legato** (i.e., bound) implies that two or more consecutive notes (or chords) are to be performed in a smooth, connected manner: and, in an extended passage, this word is sometimes written to express this effect. Much more frequently, however, a curved line, ⌒ or ⌣ (called a slur) is used, and it is understood that all notes included within such curve are to be played legato, e.g.:—

10.—In the first of the above examples, it will be noticed that the two C's at the commencement of the passage are joined by a small curve. When two notes of the same pitch are so connected, the curve is not a "slur," but a tie (or "bind") and indicates that only the first of such notes is to be struck, but that this is to be prolonged by the value of the second. This same rule would hold good, whatever number of notes were tied together, e.g.:—

In every case the prolonged sound is equal in duration to that of all the notes so tied together.

Occasionally, in the works of Beethoven and Chopin, two notes of the same pitch are connected by a curved line, the second of the two having a "staccato" mark over it, thus:—

Beethoven.—Sonata, Op. 110.

Chopin.—Valse, Op. 34, No. 1,

In such cases they are not intended to be tied. The first note is to be played with the usual amount of tone, and connected closely with the second, which is played with a much diminished tone—producing somewhat of the effect of an echo. This was originally a "grace" connected with the old clavichord, and it is not possible to reproduce it accurately on the modern Pianoforte, although the above-named writers have sought to imitate it in this way. It was entitled the "Bebung."

11.—When, in contradistinction to legato, notes are to be detached from one another, and played or sung in a short, crisp, manner, the effect so produced is called staccato.

There are three kinds of staccato in general use, indicated by one of the following signs placed over (or under) the notes desired to be so performed:—

(i.) By a dash:—

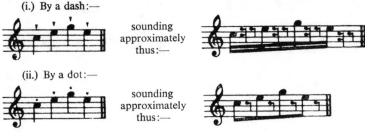

sounding approximately thus:—

(ii.) By a dot:—

sounding approximately thus:—

(iii.) By a dot combined with a curve, or slur (generally termed mezzo-staccato or portamento):—

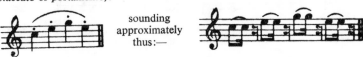

sounding approximately thus:—

12.—Two or three abbreviations, more frequently found in music for orchestral instruments than in that written for the pianoforte or organ, remain to be noticed.

(i.) The signs for reiterated notes, e.g.:—

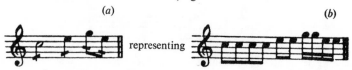

representing

One stroke through the stem of a note signifying quaver repetitions; two strokes, semiquaver repetitions; three strokes, demi-semiquaver repetitions; and so on. In the case of notes having already one or more hooks, or tails, each hook or tail counts for one stroke (See (a) above, sound as at (b)). In the case of a semibreve, the strokes are placed above or below, e.g.:—

representing

When very rapid, this effect is called tremolo.

(ii.) The signs for rapid alternations of notes, e.g. (sometimes called "legato tremolo"):—

representing

NOTE.—When two minims (or two semibreves) are joined by quaver, semiquaver, or demi-semiquaver, etc., tails, as at (c), the number of alternations is to be equal to the value of one of the written notes. (See (d).)

(iii.) The sign for repeated groups, e.g.:—

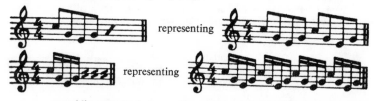

representing

representing

one oblique stroke being used as often as it is desired to repeat a group of quavers; two such strokes being similarly used in the case of semiquavers; three in the case of demi-semiquavers, and so on.

If an entire bar is to be repeated, it is often indicated thus:—

Here, in bars 2 and 3, the figure given in bar 1, is to be played twice more. Sometimes the following sign is used for the same purpose, ·/.

(iv.) A rest of greater duration than one bar is represented merely by a figure, thus:—

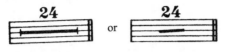

CHAPTER XI

ORNAMENTS

1.—The principal, if not the only, ornaments or graces in general use at the present day are (i.) the shake, or trill; (ii.) the turn; (iii.) the acciaccatura; (iv.) the mordent.

2.—The shake, or trill, consists of a rapid and regular alternation of a principal (written) note with the note alphabetically next above it, and is usually expressed by the letters tr. (abbreviation of the Italian trillo) above that written note, thus:—

3.—It will be seen that, in the above example, two small notes are written (the first being the note below the principal note), to form a finish to the shake; this termination is usually required (even if not indicated in writing).

4.—Sometimes, however, if the shake is followed by one or more unaccented notes, it is played without this form of termination, but care must be used that it always ends on its principal note, e.g.:—

5.—In each of these cases (Secs. 2 and 4), a triplet is introduced in order that the shake may finish on the principal note; if there is an "ending" (or "turn," as it is sometimes called), such as is described in Sec. 3, this triplet will precede it (see Ex. in Sec. 2). If, on the contrary, there is no "ending," the triplet will come immediately before the next written note. A point upon which there is some little divergence of opinion is as to whether a shake should begin upon the written note, or upon the note above.

The matter cannot be dealt with in detail here; but, generally speaking, the student may take it as a safe rule that, in modern music (except at times in that of Chopin), the shake should begin with the written note (as in the examples in Secs.

2 and 4). In the case of Haydn and Mozart, and more especially older masters, such as Bach and Handel, it is usually more appropriate to begin the shake with the upper note. This rule is inflexible when the shake is preceded by another note of the same pitch, as at (a).

Here the correct rendering would be as follows:—

The commencement of a shake upon its upper note is nowadays frequently indicated thus:—

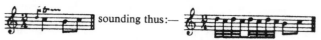

Observe that the triplet mentioned in Sec. 5 is necessary only when the shake begins on its principal note.

6.—The number of alternations of the two notes of a shake largely depends upon the speed of the music, and the length of the written note; in quick time, or in the case of a shake upon a short note, it often assumes such forms as the following:—

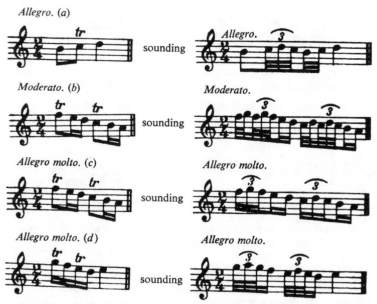

In all these cases, the character of the passage must largely influence the rendering.

7.—A ♮, ♯, ♭, × or ♭♭, over a shake shows that the note above the principal, or written one, should be inflected accordingly:—

sounding

8.—The mordent consists of a single rapid alternation of a written note and the note next alphabetically above it, and is indicated thus:— ᴡ

(a)   *Allegro.*   ᴡ   Chopin.   &c.

sounding—   &c.

(b)   *Andante.*   Bach.

sounding—

9.—The lower mordent, indicated thus ᴧ, implies a similar alternation of a principle note and the note below it, e.g.:—

Bach.   &c.

sounding—   &c.

10.—The turn, or grupetto, ∾, is an ornament consisting of four notes, played or sung after a principal, written note, as follows:—

(i.) The note above it.
(ii.) ,, written note.
(iii.) ,, note below it.
(iv.) ,, written note again.

The following example will make this clear:—

sounding

In performance, the principal note is held for a large part of its value (generally either a half in quick "tempo," and three-quarters in slow "tempo"), and the four notes of the turn occupy the remaining half, or quarter, as the case may be, e.g.:—

sounding—

Here the principal note takes one-half of its written value.

sounding—

Here the principal note takes three-quarters of its written value, to prevent the turn sounding dull and heavy.

11.—When a turn occurs after a dotted note, the written note most frequently takes half of its own value; the first three notes of the turn take the remaining half, in the form of a triplet: and its final (fourth) note has the value of the dot, e.g.:—

sounding—

N.B.—This rule admits of some relaxation occasionally in slow "tempo," and applies only to those cases in which the dot forms the beginning of a new beat, or division of a beat.

12.—When a turn is placed over a note, the turn generally begins at once with the note above the written one, e.g.:—

sounding—

but sometimes the written note is played first, and, together with the four notes of the turn, forms a group of five equal notes, e.g.:—

The character of the passage must largely determine which interpretation the turn is to bear.

13.—An accidental written under or over a turn indicates that the note below or above the written note (as the case may be) is to have a similar accidental, thus—(See also examples in Secs. 11 and 12)

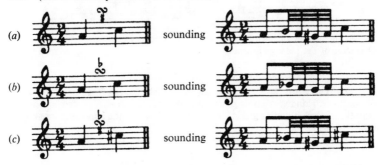

14.—An inverted turn (indicated variously by the signs ∾ ∾ and 𝒵), is a turn in which the note below the principal (written) note comes first, the note above appearing later, e.g.:—

This ornament is usually written out in full.

15.—An acciaccatura (lit., "crushing-note") is a quaver of small size, with a stroke through the stem and hook (see (a) in example below) played or sung as quickly as possible, immediately proceeding to the note before which it is placed—and from which it takes no appreciable value:—

16.—Sometimes groups of small notes are found preceding others of full-size. In such a case the group of small notes is performed more or less rapidly, the accent frequently falling on the principal note, thus:—

sounding

This rule admits, however, of many exceptions, especially in modern music; the accent often more appropriately falling on the first of the small notes, e.g.:—

Chopin.

sounding preferably—

Such niceties of performance must, of necessity, depend largely upon the character of the passage in question.

ORNAMENTS OF LESS FREQUENT OCCURRENCE

17.—There are two signs of ornaments which, though frequent in the works of Bach and Handel, are now practically obsolete, composers preferring to indicate their effect by writing them out in full. These are the appoggiatura and the extended lower mordent.

The appoggiatura (lit., leaning-note), is expressed by a small note preceding

a principal one, thus:— differing in

appearance from the acciaccatura in the absence of the stroke drawn through the stem. Moreover, an appoggiatura could be of any length,—minim, crotchet, quaver, and so on—the rule being that it should take its own value from the note that it preceded—generally one-half—as the appoggiatura was nearly always written as a small-sized note of half the value of that principal note—the appoggiatura coming upon the accent.
Thus:—

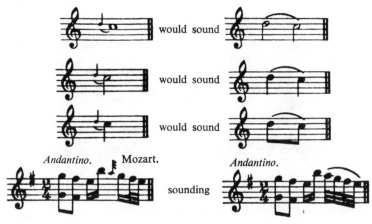

Modern composers, from Beethoven onwards, write the *appoggiatura* in full-sized notes exactly as it sounds.

18.—An appoggiatura before a dotted-note usually takes approximately two-thirds (or sometimes one-third) of the note it precedes, e.g.:—

sounding   or sometimes (rarely)

19.—The prolonged, or extended, lower mordent ⟪⟫ is an inverted (or, lower) mordent with two alternations instead of one, e.g :—

Bach.

sounding—

20.—A shake, or trill, is often found indicated in old music by one of the following signs, ⟪⟫ or ⟪⟫, a hook sometimes occurring at one end, or at both ends, e.g.:—

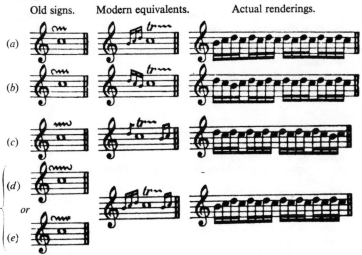

Old signs.   Modern equivalents.   Actual renderings.

(a)

(b)

(c)

(d)

or

(e)

21.—In the music of Mozart and Haydn, the turn after a dotted note is sometimes inaccurately written out in four small notes of equal length, as at (a):—

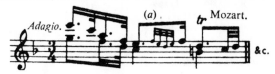

Adagio.   (a)   Mozart.

&c.

The correct rendering of such a turn would be as follows:—

Fortunately, composers are more particular nowadays as regards accuracy in expressing the effects they intend, and the meanings of the various signs employed have not to be gauged by the general tenor of the passages in which they occur.

CHAPTER XII

ITALIAN AND OTHER TERMS USED IN MUSIC

1.—The various degrees of speed and of intensity of sound, as well as directions as to the style in which passages are to be performed are generally indicated by the composer. In former times such indications were often meagre, and much was left to the good sense and taste of the executant; nowadays, however, when gradations—especially of tone—are so minute, and so important to the effect of the music, much more care is paid to the marking of the exact manner of performance.

2.—It has always been found advantageous to have these directions written in a language that should be regarded as universal, and Italian has long been used for this purpose, although some German composers, notably Schumann, have preferred to use their own native tongue, the object of which proceeding is not very clear.

3.—The following are the more frequent terms occurring in both vocal and instrumental music:—

SPEED:—

Adagio, leisurely; *Molto Adagio,* very slow.
Adagissimo, slower than *Adagio.*
Affrettando hastening the speed.
Alcuna, some; e.g. *con alcuna licenza,* with a certain degree of (i.e. some) license.
Allegro, merry, lively, fast.
Allegretto, not so fast as *Allegro.*
Andante, going at a moderate pace.
Andantino, not so slow as *Andante.*
Grave, grave, solemn.
Incalzando, increasing both in tone and speed.
Largamente,
Largo,   } broad, slow.
Larghetto, not so slow as *Largo.*
Lento, very slow.
Moderato, at a moderate pace.
Presto, quick.
Prestissimo, very quick.
Risvegliato, with animation.

Slargando,
Slentando, } getting slower.

Sopra, above.

Sotto, below, under.

Tempo comodo, in convenient time.

Tempo ordinario, in ordinary time.

Tempo primo, at the original speed.

Vivace, lively, quickly.

MODIFICATIONS OF SPEED:—

Allargando, decreasing the speed, broadening.

A tempo, in time.

Ad libitum or *A piacere,* at pleasure.

Doppio movimento, at double the pace.

L'istesso tempo, in the same time; i.e., the beats to have the same duration, however they may be expressed in notation.

Meno allegro, less fast.

Meno masso, less moved, slower.

Più mosso, more moved, quicker.

Ritardando (ritard.), holding back
Rallentando (rall.), slackening the pace } getting slower.

Ritenuto (rit.), held back, slower.

Accelerando (accel.), accelerating the pace
Stringendo, pressing onwards } getting faster.

INTENSITY OF SOUND:—

Crescendo (cres.), or < getting louder.

Decrescendo (decres.),
Diminuendo (dim.), } or > getting softer.

Forte (f.), loud.

Fortissimo (ff), very loud.

fff, as loud as possible.

Mezzo-forte (mf), half loud, or moderately loud.

Mezzo-piano (mp), half or moderately soft.

Piano (p.), soft.

Pianissimo (pp), very soft.

ppp, as soft as possible.

Dolce, softly, sweetly.

Calando, decreasing.
Mancando, waning in tone.
Morendo, dying away. } Getting slower and softer.
Perdendosi, losing itself.
Smorzando, extinguishing.

Forte piano (fp), loud, then soft
Sforzando (sf), > or ∧, forcing. } Terms used to indicate
Forzato (fz), forced. increased accent upon a single
Rinforzando (rf or rinf.), enforcing. note or chord.

OTHER TERMS RELATING TO MANNER OF PERFORMANCE:—

A, at, for, with.

A capella, in the church style.

Affettuoso, affectionately.

Agitato, in an agitated manner.

Amabile, amiably.
Amoroso, lovingly.
Animato, animated.
Appassionato, passionately.
Assai, sufficiently, very.
Attacca, go on at once.
Bene or *Ben*, well.
Ben marcato, well marked.
Brillante, brilliantly.
Brioso, with vigour.
Cantabile or *cantando*, in a singing style.
Col or *Colla*, with the.
Col arco, with the bow (applied to instruments of the violin family).
Colla parte, or *Colla voce*, keeping closely with the solo part or voice.
Come prima, as at first.
Come sopra, as above.
Con, with.
Con amore, with love.
Con anima, with soul.
Con brio, with brightness and vigour.
Con delicatezza, delicately.
Con dolore or *Con duolo*, with grief.
Con espressione, with expression.
Con energia, with energy.
Con forza, with force.
Con fuoco, with fire.
Con gracia, with grace.
Con moto, with movement.
Con sordini, with mutes (applied to instruments of the violin family). Also used occasionally (especially by Beethoven) to indicate the release of the damper pedal of the Pianoforte.
Con spirito, with spirit.
Con tenerezza, with tenderness.
Da capo, from the beginning.
Dal segno, from the sign.
Deciso, decidedly.
Delicamente or *Delicato*, delicately.
Dolce, sweetly.
Dolente, or *Doloroso*, sadly, with grief.
E or *Ed*, and.
Energico, with energy or force.
Espressivo, with expression.
Forza, force.
Fuoco, fire.
Furioso, impetuously; with fury.
Giocoso, or *Giocosamente*, gaily, jocosely.
Giojoso, joyously.
Giusto, exact.
Grandioso, grandly.
Grazioso, gracefully.
Il or *La*, the.
Impetuoso, impetuously.
Legato, smoothly; bound.
Leggiero or *Leggieramente*, lightly.

Lusingando, soothingly.
Ma, but.
Maestoso, majestically.
Maggiore, major.
Main droite (Fr.), or *M.D.*,   }
Mano destra (Ital.), or *M.D.*, } with the right hand.
Main gauche (Fr.), or *M.G.*,   }
Mano sinistra (Ital.), or *M.S.*, } with the left hand.
Marcato, marked.
Martellato, with great force; hammered.
Meno, less.
Mesto, sadly.
Mezzo, half; *mezza voce*, half voice, in an undertone.
Minore, minor.
Molto or *Di molto*, much; very.
Mosso or *Moto*, movement.
Non, not.
Parlando or *Parlante*, in a speaking manner.
Pastorale, in a pastoral style.
Ped. (abbreviation of *pedale*), indicates the use of the right, or damper, pedal of the Pianoforte.
Pesante, heavily.
Piacevole, pleasantly.
Piangevole, plaintively.
Più, more.
Più tosto, rather more quickly.
Pizzicato (*pizz.*), plucking the string (applied to bowed instruments).
Poco or *Un poco*, a little.
Poco a poco, little by little.
Poi, then.
Pomposo, pompously.
Portamento, implies the extremest smoothness (or carrying) from one note to another in singing.
Quasi, almost, as if; e.g., *Quasi una fantasia* (Beethoven), as if in the style of a fantasia.
Replica, repeat.
Risoluto, resolutely.
Scherzando or *Scherzoso*, in a sprightly, playful manner.
Sciolto, freely, easily.
Sec. (Fr., lit., dry), short, crisp.
Segue, follow on at once.
Semplice, simply.
Sempre, always.
Senza, without; *senza sordini*, without mutes (applied to instruments of the violin family). Also sometimes used to indicate the depression of the damper pedal of the Pianoforte.
Serioso, seriously.
Simile, in the same manner.
Soave, sweetly, gently.
Sostenuto, sustained.
Sotto voce, in a subdued manner; lit., under the voice.
Staccato, short and detached.
Strepitoso, in a loud, boisterous manner.
Sul ponticello, near the bridge (applied to bowed-instruments).

Tacet, be silent.

Tanto, so much.

Tempo rubato, robbed time; the slight alterations of speed which a performer makes for the purpose of expression in particular passages.

Tenuta, Tenute, Tenuto, held on, sustained.

Tranquillo or *Tranquillamente*, tranquilly.

Tre corde (lit., three strings), signifies the release of the left, or soft pedal.

Troppo, too; too much. *Non troppo*, not too much.

Un or *una*, one.

Una corda (lit., one string), signifies the use of the left, or soft, pedal of the Pianoforte.

Veloce, rapidly.

Vigoroso, vigorously.

Vivo or *Con vivacità*, with vivacity.

Volante, in a light, flying manner.

Volti subito or *V.S.*, turn over quickly.

GERMAN TERMS

Aber, but.

Ausdrucksvoll, with expression.

Bestimmt, with decision.

Beweglich, with movement: the equivalent of *con moto* in Italian.

Bewegt, moved.

Bogen, with the bow, the equivalent of *arco* or *col arco* in Italian.

Breit, broadly.

Doch, but, yet.

Einfach, simply.

Etwas, some, somewhat; e.g., *etwas bewegt*, somewhat moved.

Gebunden, connected.

Gehalten, sustained.

Gestossen, short, detached; the equivalent of *Staccato* in Italian.

Geschwind, quickly.

Immer, always.

Kräftig, with energy.

Kurz, short.

Langsam, slowly.

Lebhaft, lively.

Leicht, lightly.

Leise, lightly, softly.

Markirt, marked.

Mässig, moderate; e.g. *mässig bewegt*, moderately moved, or moderately quickly.

Mit, with.

Munter, lively; the equivalent of *Allegro* in Italian.

Nicht, not.

Noch, still more; e.g. *noch schneller*, still quicker.

Rasch, quickly.

Ruhig, calmly.

Schnell, quickly; *so schnell wie möglich*, as quickly as possible.

Sehr, very.

Stark, strongly.

Und, and

Wenig, little, e.g., *ein wenig langsamer*, a little slower.

Zart, soft.

Ziemlich, rather moderately.

Zu, too.

CHAPTER XIII

HARMONY

1.—Broadly, the study of Harmony may be said to be concerned with—
   (*a*) The combination of musical sounds into what are usually spoken of as chords;
   (*b*) The classification of such chords;
   (*c*) The relation of such chords to one another, particularly as to the various ways in which they may succeed each other.

2.—Closely connected with, and inseparable from, these are—
   (*a*) Melody (or tune),
   (*b*) Rhythm (the intelligent division of music into periods or sentences), two important factors in modern musical composition, without which Harmony alone would be dead and meaningless.

3.—When two or more musical sounds are sung or played together, a chord is produced, and the simplest kind of complete chord is formed by taking a bass-note, and adding to it its 3rd and 5th; e.g.:—

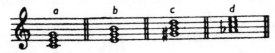

This is called a Triad.

4.—The above example will show that the quality of 3rd and 5th so added may vary. As a matter of fact, either a major or minor 3rd may be used, and either a perfect, diminished, or augmented 5th.

5.—When a triad has a perfect 5th, it is called a common chord. Common chords may have a major or minor 3rd, when they are described as major or minor common chords respectively, e.g.:—

6.—Common chords (either major or minor) are concordant triads, because they are satisfactory in themselves and need no other chord to follow them.

7.—When a triad has a diminished 5th, it always takes with it a minor 3rd, and is called a diminished triad, e.g.:—

and when it has an augmented 5th, it always takes with it a major 3rd and is called an augmented triad, e.g.:—

8.—Diminished and augmented triads are termed discordant, or dissonant triads, as they seem to require some other chord to follow them, to complete their effect.

9.—An inversion of a chord is produced by placing any other note than its root (i.e., the note from which it is derived, and from which it takes its name) in the bass; e g :—

Direct chord   First inversion   Second inversion

(Root in bass.)   (3rd in bass.)   (5th in bass.)

10.—Chords are found with their notes placed in various orders, and they may be embellished by the addition of ornamental notes called passing-notes, suspensions, etc.—all of which will be spoken of later.

11.—It must be understood also that, in actual composition, chords are frequently found in a broken form (i.e., with their notes dispersed in "arpeggiated" and other figures), e.g. :—

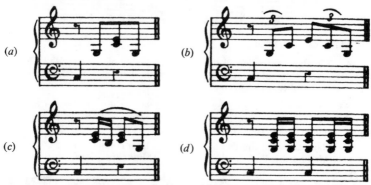

These, and many others that might be given, are all variations upon the chord—

which, in itself, is merely a fuller aspect of the common chord marked (a) in Sec. 3 above, caused by writing the bass-note an 8ve lower, and doubling it (see Sec. 13) and by placing the 3rd of the chord at the top, and the 5th next to the bass-note.

12.—Chords are mostly written in four parts—the most complete and satisfactory effect being usually obtainable thus, when written for voices.

13.—When four voices sing a triad, one of the notes is always doubled, i.e., used twice in the same chord:—

&c.

When a chord is direct, this is nearly always the root, as in the above example; in the case of a 1st inversion, either the 3rd or the 6th from the bass-note is doubled, usually, thus:—

while, in a 2nd inversion, the bass-note is by far the best note to double, e.g.:—

The position of the root of the chord as a 4th above the bass-note of a 2nd inversion gives somewhat of the effect of a discord, requiring some other chord to succeed. This accounts for the fact of a 2nd inversion of a triad being always followed in a definite way. Its most usual progression is to a direct common chord upon the same bass-note, e.g.:—

14.—Here is a table, showing the position of the various triads, and their inversions, in both major and minor forms of a key.

Major Common Chords are written as white notes.

Minor Common Chords are written as black notes.

Diminished and Augmented Triads in small type, in brackets.

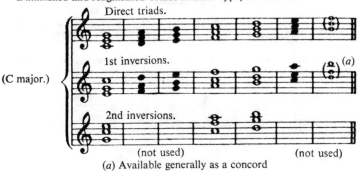

(a) Available generally as a concord

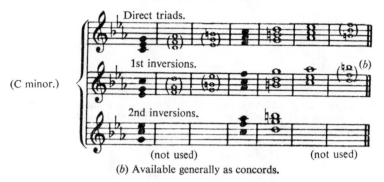

(C minor.)

(b) Available generally as concords.

15.—The Chord of the Dominant 7th is formed by adding a minor 7th to the common chord on the Dominant of any scale, e.g.:—

It is a discord and consequently requires resolution, i.e., a fixed, definite progression. It most usually resolves upon the common chord of the Tonic, thus:—

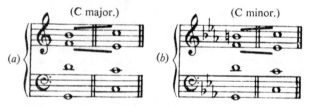

the 3rd of the Dominant 7th chord rising one semitone, and the 7th falling a 2nd (major or minor).

It has 3 inversions, as follows:—

16.—The addition of 3rds to the chord of the Dominant 7th produces the chords often spoke of as the Dominant 9th, 11th, and 13th, thus:—

The small notes in brackets are generally omitted.
Here are some frequent examples of these chords:—

(i.) Chord of the Dominant 9th.

The 9th may be either a major or a minor 9th in the major form of a key: in the minor form, the 9th is minor.

(ii.) Chord of the Dominant 11th.

(11th.)   (9th and 11th.)

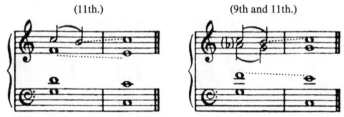

(iii.) Chord of the Dominant 13th.

(13th.)   (9th and 13th.)   (11th and 13th.)

In the minor form of a key, the 13th is minor.

All these chords may be taken in their various inversions, the note upon which the 9th, 11th, or 13th resolves being nearly always omitted from the chord, e.g. :—

Dominant 9th   Dominant 11th   Dominant 13th
(1st inversion).   (2nd inversions).   (3rd inversion).

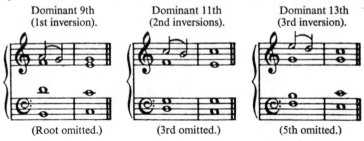

(Root omitted.)   (3rd omitted.)   (5th omitted.)

17.—All these examples can be taken in the minor mode of the key, with the substitution of a minor 9th and a minor 13th for the major 9th and 13th, respectively.

18.—Modulation, or change of key, takes place when a chord not in the original key is introduced, and followed by another chord, or chords, defining the new key, e.g.:—

19.—A chromatic chord is a chord that contains one or more notes needing accidentals, but which does not change the key, e.g.:—

Chromatic chord.

20.—The following specially-named chords are often met with:—

(i.) The "Neapolitan 6th."
(ii.) The "Italian 6th."
(iii.) The "French 6th."   } Varieties of one chord.
(iv.) The "German 6th."
(v.) The "Added 6th"

The Neapolitan 6th is the first inversion of a chromatic major common chord upon the minor 2nd of the scale, e.g.:—

The Italian, French, and German 6ths are the three forms of the chord of the Augmented 6th, occurring most usually upon the minor 6th of a scale, and resolving generally either upon the common chord of the Tonic or the Dominant, e.g.:—

x Italian 6th. x French 6th.

x German 6th.

The Added 6th is the first inversion of a chord of the 7th formed diatonically upon the supertonic of a key—usually called a secondary 7th, e.g.:—

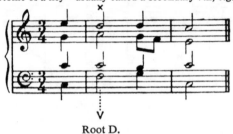

Root D.

21.—Passing-notes are notes used to fill the gaps, so to speak, in passing from one note of a chord to another, as at (*a*), or from a note of one chord to a note of another chord, as at (*b*):—

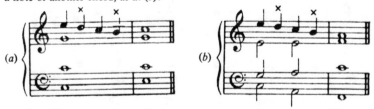

(*a*) (*b*)

Sometimes a passing-note is struck with the chord, when it is called an Accented Passing-note, or Appoggiatura, e.g.:—

Passing-notes are foreign to the chords against which they are taken, and are therefore termed unessential discords. They are usually approached and quitted by the step of a 2nd.

22.—Another class of unessential discord is formed by Suspensions. A Suspension is the prolonging of a note of one chord while another chord is being sounded, of which that note forms no part. The note so retained moves by the descent or ascent of a 2nd to a note of the chord over which it has been held. The following examples will make this clear. Here is a passage of simple harmony:—

By the delaying of certain of the notes, suspensions can be introduced, thus:—

Suspensions take their names from the distance at which they stand from the root of the chord; consequently the suspension at (a) is a suspended 6th; that at (b) a suspended 9th; and those at (c), (d), (e) or (f) are suspended 4ths.

23.—A Sequence is the repetition of a progression of melody or harmony upon other degrees of the scale, e.g.:—

24.—A Pedal, or Pedal-note is a note, usually in the bass, sustained through a succession of harmonies, of which it may, or may not, form a part, e.g.:—

The notes almost exclusively used as Pedals are the Dominant and the Tonic of any key. The above example shows an instance of a Dominant Pedal.

25.—A Cadence is the completion of a phrase, or rhythmical period. There are four principal cadences, viz.:—

    (*a*) The Perfect (or Authentic) Cadence, when a phrase ends with the Tonic chord, preceded by that of the Dominant;

    (*b*) The Imperfect (or Half) Cadence, when a phrase ends with the chord of the Dominant;

    (*c*) The Interrupted Cadence, when the course of the music leads one to expect a perfect cadence, but when some other chord is substituted for that of the Tonic: often that of the Sub-mediant;

    (*d*) The Plagal Cadence, when a phrase ends with the chord of the Tonic, preceded by that of the Sub-dominant.

26.—When figures are found under a bass-note, they indicate the intervals of the chord counted from that bass-note, e.g.:—

where the root of the chord, C, is a 4th above the bass, and the 3rd of the chord, E, is the 6th above the bass. The figuring of the simpler chords (viz., triads and the Dominant 7th) is as follows:—

Triads and their Inversions.

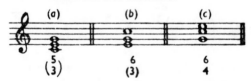

The chord marked (*b*) is thus often called a chord of the sixth, while that at (*c*) is described as a chord of the six-four.

Dominant 7th and its Inversions.

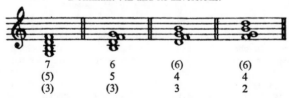

The figures in brackets are usually omitted.

An accidental placed before a figure indicates that the note represented by that figure is to have a similar accidental, e.g.:—

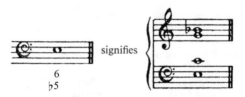

27.—It is not possible, within the limits of the present primer, to enter more fully into the question of the various chords, etc., described in this Chapter, nor can any attempt be here made to set forth the laws that govern their treatment. The student who desires to prosecute this most important subject can do so by referring to the author's "Practical Harmony," (Galliard Ltd) where he will find all these matters exhaustively considered.

CHAPTER XIV

MODERN DEVELOPMENTS IN MELODY, HARMONY, AND RHYTHM

1.—Much of the music of the present century uses procedures rather different from those tabulated in the previous chapters, and many of these stemmed from an increasing employment by earlier composers, such as Wagner, of the notes of the chromatic scale (described in Chapter VIII). In fact to make their melodies more expressive, composers began to use as many chromatic notes as diatonic notes in the key of the melody. These chromatic notes follow on logically from the idea of passing notes explained in Chapter XIII. They are a more colourful way of "filling in the gaps". The following tune by Wagner is really in F sharp minor and the starred notes are chromatic passing notes.

2.—At the same time composers began to employ more disjointed shapes in their melodies, using wider intervals like this theme from Mahler's Ninth Symphony. Again the reason was to gain in expressiveness and tension.

3.—Just as we find more chromatic notes in the melodies, so we find a greater use of chromatic chords filling in the gaps between those that belong to the key of the passage in question. Chords like the Augmented Sixth illustrated in Chapter XIII, as well as dominant discords which have been temporarily borrowed from other keys. Also the harmonies themselves begin to look and sound less like the ones we have learned about earlier in the book. Often this is because the chromatic passing notes between chords have become incorporated into the chord itself. The following example gives a simple explanation for a rich and complex chord.

4.—The colourful nature of this kind of harmony became so attractive to composers that passages like the following became standard. The melody is in G (Dorian mode) but very few of the harmonies belong to that key.

A complicated explanation for such harmonies could be made according to the old rules. But it seems more sensible to understand them as beautiful sounds which have been joined together like colourful beads on a string.

5.—It can be seen that the harmony in the above passage is a long way from any single key or diatonic scale. It uses all the twelve notes of the chromatic scale quite freely, and only returns positively to the key of G at the end.

The next step towards modern methods was taken when composers began to be satisfied with these beautiful chromatic harmonies for their sake, and felt that any references to a key were unnecessary. At the same time their interest in the pure sound of chords like the one in section 3 led them to experiment with building new chords which could not be found in the old key system. Chords which were no longer built in thirds like those in Chapter VIII, or ones which (following logically the procedure in section 3) incorporated so many passing notes that they became totally different from the original.

Schoenberg, for instance, used in his *First Chamber Symphony* a chord built out of fourths.

Scriabin invented a chord which he thought had mystical qualities.

While Debussy built chords out of the whole-tone scale—a scale which together with the chromatic provides an alternative to the major and minor As its name implies it is constructed entirely out of tones.

Debussy builds chords from it like the following.

A further procedure found in many composers is the simultaneous combinaion of harmonies from two keys (bi-tonality) as in this example from Stravinsky's *Rite of Spring*.

All these different methods flouted the conventions of previous music, and in most cases all that the composers had to guide them was their sixth sense as to what made interesting sound.

6 —Some composers, however, eventually felt the need to be more systematic about their harmony and melody. One of the most important of these was Schoenberg, whose twelve note method became the basis of many modern masterpieces By this method the composer constructs his melodies and harmonies out of a basic series of notes. This series or row places the twelve notes of the chromatic scale in a certain order, and obviously the practical composer chooses an order which will enable him to write the sort of melodies and harmonies he wants. By returning also to the methods of Bach and much earlier composers who used to vary their melodies by reversing them, inverting them, or even reversing the inversion, Schoenberg evolved the method of working with four forms of his basic series, the Original (sometimes called Prime), Inversion, Retrograde and Retrograde–Inversion. Each of these forms can be transposed to start on any note of the chromatic scale, so that the composer has at his disposal 48 forms of his basic series to work with in any one piece This is the row which Schoenberg used for his *Variations for Orchestra* together with its Inversion, Retrograde and Retrograde–Inversion (the four forms are normally abbreviated as O, I, R, RI).

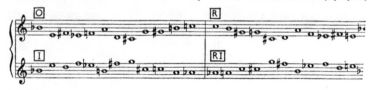

And this is how he derives the work's main theme and its harmony from it.

In that example two forms of the row were used, one for the melody, one for the accompaniment. One row form can also do the same amount of work as in this theme from Schoenberg's *Suite Op* 29.

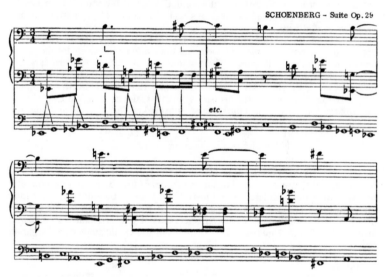

The previous example also provides an answer to the important question of what the composer does when he has used up his twelve notes. Here he continues with another form of the row which begins with the same note or two notes that closed the previous bar. In the first bar he uses O on E flat, in the second R on E flat, in the third I on E flat, and in the fourth RI on E flat.

Finally to hint at how many different kinds of music you can compose with note rows, here is a passage from Berg's Violin Concerto. This work uses a row which produces more traditional sounding harmony.

BERG – Violin Concerto

O on G

N.b. The E and C have been reversed by the composer, an indication that the note order of a
     series need not be too strictly adhered to.

In post-script it should be said that twelve-note writing is the orthodox method
of serial composition. Stravinsky, however, uses a five note row in his *In Memoriam
Dylan Thomas*, and other lengths of row have also been employed. And the Greek
composer Skalkottas evolved a method of working with several entirely different
basic rows to a work, each with its 48 different versions, so that the possibilities of
the method can be seen to be enormous.

7.—Obviously enough not all composers have subscribed to serial systems.
Hindemith, for instance, worked out a method based on the acoustical properties
of intervals, and governed the tensions and relaxations of his harmonies and
melodies in that way.

Others continued to compose in a more traditional way like Bartok, whose
highly characteristic chords and melodies were often influenced by the exotic
modes of his native folk music. These sound very strange to Western ears: the
major scale with an augmented fifth and minor seventh, the minor with an augmented fourth, or else with a flattened second, diminished fourth and minor
sixth. Bartok also constructed his own synthetic scales as a logical extension of
the folk modes. This for instance is used in his ballet *The Miraculous Mandarin*.

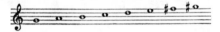

8.—Just as composers began to use all the chromatic notes in melody and
harmony, and to use wider intervals in the shapes of themes, so they also found it
necessary to employ different types of rhythm, because they did not want their
music to move forward with a regular pulse. A simple example of this is to be
heard in Bartok's *Fifth String Quartet* where bars of $\frac{9}{8}$ are irregularly split up into
groups of 4, 2 and 3 quavers. This stems from the exotic steps of a Bulgarian
dance.

Vivace   BARTOK – String Quartet No.5

In that example the composer used regular series of bars even if the grouping
of notes within these bars was irregular. Another rhythmic method is to use
irregular series of bars each with a different time signature. This has been called

additive rhythm, because there is no regular pulse, merely a continual adding on of different length bars as in this movement of Tippett's *Second String Quartet.*

A further factor in the growing rhythmic complexity of modern music has been a growth in the use of "irrational values" or triplets, quadruplets, quin-tuplets etc. The use of such groups of notes in conjunction with irregular bars produces very complicated results. Notes fall on all sorts of fractions of the beat and pulse, either regular or irregular, disappears. This kind of music does not move purposefuly forward any more, but remains still for our contemplation.

STOCKHAUSEN – Piano Piece No. 2

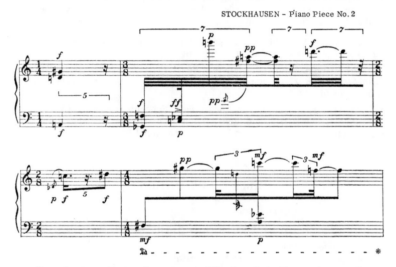

In order to get over the extreme difficulty of reading such complicated notation, some composers have devised simpler methods for producing a rhyth-mic result as complex as that in the above passage. There is for instance the spatial method where the player judges the rhythm from the position of the notes within the bar.

This is obviously a free method as no two players will make exactly the same decision, while during a single performance the differing interpretations by each performer of his part will produce minute rhythmic subtleties without undue difficulty. The composer exercises control over the rhythm by indicating places where the players must come exactly together. These points are usually shown by arrows.

9.—Another natural development from the music of extreme melodic and rhythmic complexity dealt with above was the employment of mechanical elec-tronic means to produce sounds which no human being could play. Working with tape and tape recorders, composers could experiment with sounds, speeding them up, slowing them down, raising or lowering the pitch by fractional amounts, playing them backwards etc. While by joining various accurately measured lengths of tape, they could organise the note lengths (rhythm) more precisely and minutely than any human performer could calculate. And by using electronically produced sounds rather than those made by instrumentalists, composers could work with a range of timbres and sonorities quite different from those of the symphony orchestra and more directly controllable by them. To manipulate these thousands of possibilities in rhythm, pitch and colours of sound, mathematical techniques have been used and some composers have been aided by computers.

Already many different types of music have been produced by electronic means. The Italian composer Berio's *Visage* is entirely built on tape from noises made by one singer which have been distorted, transformed, cut up, re-assembled and constructed into an almost symphonic work. Stockhausen has written pieces in which live performers play into microphones, and an operator distorts their sounds with electronic equipment, broadcasting the result to the audience at the same time as the live performance is going on. Other pieces exist on tape like *Visage* but have been entirely made out of electronic sound, while others again combine a part for tape and recorder with one for players. It is a rapidly expanding field and will certainly play an important part in the history of music.

The extract from Michael Tippett's *Second String Quartet* is reproduced by kind permission of Schott and Co. Ltd., the copyright holders.

The extracts from Stockhausen's *Piano Piece No. 2* and from Bartok's *Fifth String Quartet* are reproduced by kind permission of Universal Edition (London) Ltd.

The extracts from Delius' *Brigg Fair*, Schoenberg's *Suite Op. 29* and *Variations for Orchestra*, and Berg's *Violin Concerto* are reproduced by kind permission of Universal Edition (Alfred A. Kalmus Ltd.)

TABLE OF DEFINITIONS

Accent.—Stress or emphasis.

Acciaccatura.—A small note, indicated ♪ , to be played as closely as possible to the full-sized note it precedes.

Accidental.—A ♮, ♯, ♭, × or ♭♭ occurring incidentally.

Agrémens (Fr.).—Ornaments, e.g., the turn, the mordent, etc.

Air.—Melody or tune.

Alla Breve.—A time consisting of four minims in a bar $\left(\frac{4}{2}\right)$, the bar being consequently of the value of one breve. Often incorrectly applied to a bar of duple time, consisting of two minims, indicated thus:—₵.

Alto clef.—The C clef 𝄡 , or 𝄡 , so placed that "Middle C" occurs as the 3rd line of a staff, thus:— --𝄡

Alto voice.—The voice next below the treble in a choir or quartet of voices; usually called contralto when sung by women. Average compass—

Appoggiatura.—A small note, placed before one of full size, and taking its own value from it. Nowadays always incorporated in the time of the bar.

Arpeggio.—The notes of a chord sounded in succession.

B (German).—The note B flat.

Bar.—The music comprised between two successive strongest accents.

Bar-line.—A vertical line drawn through the staff immediately before the constantly recurring strongest accent.

Baritone voice.—A voice lighter than a Bass, but fuller than a Tenor.

with a compass between the two, approximately—

Bass clef.—The F clef.

Bass note.—The lowest note in any chord

Bass voice.—The lowest male voice. Average compass—

Beat.—One of the main divisions of a bar, or measure.

Bémol (French
Bémolle (Italian) } a flat; e.g., Fa bémol or Fa bémolle, signifies F flat.

Bind.—See *Tie.*

Cadence.—The completion of a phrase, or rhythmical period.

Chord.—Two or more notes sounded together.

Chromatic.—Notes contrary to the key-signature, without causing modulation.

Chromatic chord.—A chord containing one or more such notes.

Chromatic interval.—An interval found only in a chromatic scale.

Chromatic scale.—A scale proceeding entirely by semitones.

Chromatic semitone.—A semitone, the two notes of which bear the same letter-name, e.g., C to C♯.

Clef.—A sign used to fix the absolute pitch of the notes upon a staff.

Common Chord.—A chord, consisting of a bass-note, with its major or minor 3rd and perfect 5th.

Common Time.—A term sometimes used to denote either Duple or Quadruple time.

Compound interval.—An interval greater than an octave (e.g., a 9th, 10th; etc.).

Compound times.—Times, in which each beat of a bar is divisible by three, as opposed to simple times, in which each beat is divisible by two.

Concord.—A combination of notes satisfactory in itself. needing no other to precede or follow it.

Consonant, or *Concordant intervals.*—The intervals of major and minor 3rd and 6th, and all perfect intervals (except occasionally the perfect 4th).

Contralto voice.—See *Alto.*

Counterpoint.—The art of combining separate melodies, or of making vocal or instrumental parts move melodiously one against another.

Couplet.—A group of two notes, to be performed in the time of three of the same quality, indicated by the figure 2 placed over or under the group, thus:—

Diapason normal.—The standard of pitch, known as French pitch, regulated

on the principle of representing a sound of 522 vibrations per second.

Diatonic.—Notes according to the key-signature. *N.B.*—The major 6th and 7th of a minor scale are, moreover, diatonic, although it is necessary to indicate them by the use of accidentals.

Diatonic chord.—A chord containing only diatonic notes.

Diatonic interval.—An interval that can be found in any major or minor scale.

Diatonic scale.—A scale proceeding by tones and semitones, in a definite order.

Diatonic semitone.—A semitone, the two notes of which bear different letter-names, e.g., C to D flat.

Dièse (French)
Diesis (Italian) } a sharp; e.g., *Fa dièse* or *Fa diesis* signifies F sharp.

Discord.—A combination of notes incomplete in itself and requiring some other to follow (and sometimes to precede) it.

Dissonant or discordant intervals.—All intervals of 2nd, 7th and 9th, and all diminished and augmented intervals.

Divisi.—A term used in writing for the bowed-instruments in an orchestra, indicating the division of any particular section (e.g., first violins, second violins, etc.) into two or more separate parts.

Do.—The Italian vocal syllable used to denote C.

Dominant.—The name given to the 5th degree of a diatonic scale.

Double-bar.—Two vertical lines drawn through the staff to indicate the termination of a section of a movement.

Duple.—A term used to describe the species of time containing two beats, or divisions, in each bar.

Dur.—The German term for a major key, e.g., *C dur* signifies C major.

Enharmonic.—Change of name without change of pitch; e.g., D♯, E♭ and F♭♭ are the enharmonic of one another.

Es (German).—A syllable affixed to the letter-name of any note, to signify the flattening of that note.

Extended mordent.—A lower mordent with two alternations instead of one. See *Mordent.*

Extreme parts.—The highest and lowest notes of a chord; e.g., those sung by the Soprano and Bass voices.

Fa.—The Italian vocal syllable used to denote F.

Full score.—The parts for an orchestra (with or without voices) placed one above another on the same page.

Gamut.—The scale.

Glissando.—Gliding; applied to the rapid sliding of the fingers over several keys in Pianoforte playing, or over several strings in Harp playing.

Graces.—Musical ornaments.

Great staff.—A staff of eleven lines, including, roughly, the average compass of both male and female voices.

H (German).—The note B natural.

Harmonics.—Sounds produced by the fact of a string or column of air vibrating in its fractional parts, as well as in its whole length.

Harmony.—Sounds in combination.

Inflection.—The alteration of the pitch of a note by the addition of an accidental.

Interval.—The difference in pitch between two sounds.

Inversion:—

(i.) Of an interval; the changing of the relative position of the two notes.

(ii.) Of a chord; the placing of any note of the chord, other than its root, in the bass or lowest part.

Is (German).—A syllable affixed to the letter-name of any note, to signify the sharpening of that note.

Key.—A set of notes (diatonic and chromatic) having a definite relation to a particular starting-point, or *key-note* (q.v.).

Key-note.—The note forming the starting point of any scale.

Key-signature.—The sharps or flats necessary to the key of a composition, placed immediately after the clef, in their proper order.

La.—The Italian vocal syllable used to denote A.

Leading-note.—The 7th degree of a diatonic scale, so called from the fact that it leads the ear to expect the tonic or key-note, from which it stands at the distance of a semitone.

Ledger lines.—Short lines drawn above or below the staff.

Maggiore (Italian) ⎫ major.
Majeu (French) ⎭

Major.—(i.) As applied to intervals; a term used to qualify the intervals of 2nd, 3rd, 6th, 7th and 9th.

    (ii.) As applied to chords; a common chord having a major (or greater) 3rd.

    (iii.) As applied to scales; a scale having its semitones occurring between the 3rd and 4th, and 7th and 8th degrees.

Measure.—The music comprised between two bar-lines. (See *Bar.*)

Mediant.—The name given to the third degree of a diatonic scale.

Melody.—Single sounds in succession. Also used as synonymous with *tune.*

Mezzo-Soprano.—A voice lying between the soprano and contralto in

pitch. Average compass—

Mezzo-Soprano Clef.—The C clef 𝄡 or 𝄡 , so placed that "Middle

C" occurs as the 2nd line of a staff, thus:—

This clef is now obsolete.

Mi.—The Italian vocal syllable used to denote E.

Middle C.—The C nearest to the middle of the Pianoforte keyboard; a note capable of being sounded by all the various voices, male and female.

Mineur (French) ⎫ minor.
Minore (Italian) ⎭

Minor.—(i.) As applied to intervals; a term used to qualify the intervals of 2nd, 3rd, 6th, 7th and 9th. See also *Major.*

    (ii.) As applied to chords; a common chord having a minor (or lesser) third.

    (iii.) As applied to scales; a scale having its semitones occurring between the 2nd and 3rd, 5th and 6th, 7th and 8th degrees. This is called the Harmonic minor scale. The Melodic minor scale is somewhat differently formed.

Mode.—(i.) A term used to denote a particular aspect of a key, e.g., its major mode, or its minor mode. Thus C major and C minor are the two opposite modes of the key of C.

    (ii) An old Ecclesiastical scale. The chief of such modes, in all of which the semitones occurred between different degrees, were—

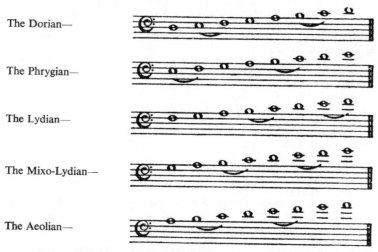

The Dorian—

The Phrygian—

The Lydian—

The Mixo-Lydian—

The Aeolian—

    (For further information on the Ecclesiastical scales, the student is recommended to the excellent article by the late Mr. W. S. Rockstro, in Grove's "Dictionary of Music and Musicians.")

Modulation.—Change of key.

Moll.—The German term for a minor key; e.g., C moll signifies C. minor.

Mordent.—A "grace" or ornament, consisting of a single rapid alternation of a written note and the note next above it, alphabetically.

Note.—A sign used to denote relative duration of sound.

Octave.—(i.) The interval of an 8th.

  (ii.) The reproduction of any note at a higher or lower pitch.

  (iii.) The sounds contained between any note and such reproduction.

Open Score.—The voice-parts of a chorus, etc., written on separate staves, one above another.

Opus (generally abbreviated thus—*Op.*); lit., a work. A term used to denote the number of a composition of any particular composer, in order of publication.

Partition (Fr.)   ⎫
Partitur (Germ.) ⎬ A score. (See *Score.*)
           ⎭

Perfect.—A term used to qualify the intervals of unison, 4th, 5th and 8th.

Phrase.—A musical period (often consisting of four bars).

Pitch.—The height or depth of a sound.

Pulse.—The measured "throb" of the music.

Quadruple.—A term used to describe the species of time containing four beats or divisions, in each bar.

Quadruplet.—A group of four notes, usually met with in compound times, to be performed in the time of six of the same quality, thus:—

The quadruplet is occasionally somewhat inaccurately treated as being equivalent to a normal group of three notes, e.g.:—

Quintuple.—A rare kind of time, having five beats, or divisions in each bar.

Quintuplet.—A group of five notes, to be performed in the time of four of the same quality, indicated by the figure 5 placed over or under the group; thus:—

Re.—The Italian vocal syllable used to denote D.

Related keys.—Keys having the greatest number of chords in common.

Relative Major ⎰ A major scale and a minor scale with the same key-
Relative Minor ⎱ signature.

Resolution.—The fixed progression of a discord.

Rest.—A sign used to denote silence for a definite period.

Rhythm.—The vital principle in music by means of which sounds are felt to "progress" to certain points of culmination or of repose, thus forming intelligible periods (such as phrases, sentences, etc.).

Root.—The note from which a chord is derived, and from which it takes its name.

Scale.—An alphabetical succession of sounds having reference to some particular starting-point, or key-note.

Score.—The parts for the various voices or instruments in a composition, placed one above another on the same page.

Semitone.—Half-a-tone. The smallest interval on the Pianoforte or Organ Keyboard.

Sentence.—A musical period (most frequently ending with a perfect cadence) consisting of two or more phrases.

Septolet.—A group of seven notes to be performed in the time of (*a*) four, or (*b*) six, of the same quality, usually indicated by the figure 7 placed over or under the group, thus:—

Sextolet.—A group of six notes to be performed in the time of four of the same quality, usually indicated by the figure 6 placed over or under the group,

thus:—

Shake.—The rapid and regular alternation of a written note with the note next above it alphabetically.

Short score.—The parts for a chorus, etc., arranged upon two staves, as for the Pianoforte.

Si.—The Italian vocal syllable used to denote B.

Signature.—See *Key-signature* and *Time-signature.*

Simple Interval.—Any interval within the octave.

Simple Times.—Times in which each beat of a bar is divisible by two.

Slur.—A sign used to indicate smoothness of performance.

Sol.—The Italian vocal syllable used to denote G.

Sol-Fa.—The use of the Italian syllables—Do, re, mi, fa, sol, la, si, in singing the notes of the scale.

Soprano.—The highest female voice. Average compass—

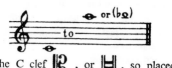

Soprano Clef.—The C clef ![clef], or ![clef], so placed that "Middle C" occurs as the 1st line of a staff, thus:—

Staff (or Stave).—The lines and spaces used to fix the relative pitch of sounds.

Subdominant.—The name given to the 4th degree of a diatonic scale.

Submediant.—The name given to the 6th degree of a diatonic scale.

Supertonic.—The name given to the 2nd degree of a diatonic scale.

Syncopation.—A disturbance of the normal accent of a bar.

Tempo (Italian).—The speed of a composition.

Tenor.—A high male voice of a comparatively light quality. Average

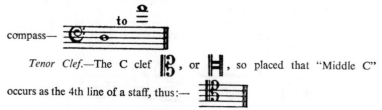

compass—

Tenor Clef.—The C clef ![clef], or ![clef], so placed that "Middle C" occurs as the 4th line of a staff, thus:—

Tetrachord.—A series of four notes in alphabetical order, most frequently consisting of two tones and a semitone.

Tie.—A curved line, ⌒ or ⌣, connecting two or more notes of the same letter-name and quality (as sharp, flat, natural, etc.), indicating that the first of such notes only is to be struck, and then prolonged by the value of the note or notes with which it is so connected.

Timbre (Fr.).—Quality of tone.

Time.—The grouping of sounds into sets by means of accent.

Time-signature.—Figures in fractional form (thus $\frac{2}{4}$, $\frac{3}{8}$, $\frac{12}{16}$, etc.) placed at the commencement of a piece to indicate the position of the accents, i.e., the time in which the piece is written.

Tonic.—The name given to the 1st degree, or keynote, of a scale.

Tonic Major.—⎱ A Major scale and a Minor scale, beginning upon the
Tonic Minor.—⎰ same tonic, or key note.

Treble.—Another name for the soprano voice. (See *Soprano.*)

Treble Clef.—The G clef.

Triad.—A chord consisting of a bass note, with its major or minor 3rd, and diminished, perfect, or augmented 5th.

Trill.—Another name for a shake. (See *Shake.*)

Triple.—A term used to describe the species of time containing three beats, or divisions, in each bar.

Triplet.—A group of three equal notes performed in the time of two of the same quality. The figure 3 is usually placed over such a group, when it occurs

incidentally, thus:—

Tritone.—(lit., three tones) the step from the 4th to the 7th degree of a diatonic scale, e.g.:—

(In C major.)

forming the interval of augmented 4th.

Turn.—A musical ornament, consisting of four notes, played or sung after a principal, written, note.

Tutti.—All. A term used, principally in orchestral music, to denote that the whole body of performers is to play.

Unison.—The same sound produced by two or more voices or instruments. Male and female voices, when they sing in octaves, are described (inaccurately) as singing in unison.

Vocal Score.—Vocal parts ranged one above another on the same page.

TABLE OF NAMES OF NOTES

English.	Italian.	French.	German.
C (natural)	Do	Ut	C
C sharp	Do diesis	Ut dièse	Cis
C flat	Do bemolle	Ut bémol	Ces
D	Re	Re	D
D sharp	Re diesis	Re dièse	Dis
D flat	Re bemolle	Re bémol	Des
E	Mi	Mi	E
E sharp	Mi diesis	Mi dièse	Eis
E flat	Mi bemolle	Mi bémol	Es
F	Fa	Fa	F
F sharp	Fa diesis	Fa dièse	Fis
F flat	Fa bemolle	Fa bémol	Fes
G	Sol	Sol	G
G sharp	Sol diesis	Sol dièse	Gis
G flat	Sol bemolle	Sol bémol	Ges
A	La	La	A
A sharp	La diesis	La dièse	Ais
A flat	La bemolle	La bémol	As
B	Si	Si	H
B sharp	Si diesis	Si dièse	His
B flat	Si bemolle	Si bémol	B

PLACING OF KEY SIGNATURES

The following examples will indicate the method of placing sharps and flats on the Staff when the C and F clefs are used:—

Soprano.   Alto.   Tenor.   Bass.

Printed in Great Britain by Galliard (Printers) Ltd Great Yarmouth